"J-Mac rocks! His book rocks! I have autism like him. But I am not autism. He makes me proud and he showed me I could do great things with my life even when somebody tells me I cannot."

—R. J. Peete, Son of Holly Robinson Peete and Rodney Peete

Praise for
The Game of My Life

"The Indianapolis Colts got to know Jason McElwain during our 2006 season when he worked for us as a ball boy in training camp. Jason is a tremendous young man who happens to be autistic. I learned a lot from him, and I learned even more from his book. *The Game of My Life* tells how he became nationally known, but it is much more than a story about one game. It talks about autism, about life, and about how much can be accomplished by having a great attitude and 'staying focused.'"

—Tony Dungy, Head Coach, Indianapolis Colts

"A lot of us feel like this is our gift, to have this happen and to have it receive so much nationwide publicity. There are thousands of Jasons out there, carrying the net for the soccer team, keeping statistics for the baseball team, playing the drum for the school band. This serves as a reminder to give these kids a chance whenever possible."

—Dr. Catherine Lord, Director of the
University of Michigan's Autism and
Communications Disorders Center

"A winning and inspiring story. . . . The most remarkable thing about the book is that it is mostly told in J-Mac's own words. . . . It's a story about being autistic, told directly from the heart, and it punches through the usual psychobabble and analytic blather to the straightforward truths . . . a deeply affecting, enlightening, and engaging book." —*Booklist* (Starred Review)

"Inspiring." —*Kirkus Reviews*

"McElwain's book spoke right to my heart. . . . [His] words of determination . . . resonate through the book." —*The Boston Globe*

THE GAME OF MY LIFE

A True Story of Challenge,
Triumph, and Growing Up Autistic

Jason "J-Mac" McElwain
with Daniel Paisner

 NEW AMERICAN LIBRARY

New American Library
Published by New American Library, a division of
Penguin Group (USA) Inc., 375 Hudson Street,
New York, New York 10014, USA
Penguin Group (Canada), 90 Eglinton Avenue East, Suite 700, Toronto,
Ontario M4P 2Y3, Canada (a division of Pearson Penguin Canada Inc.)
Penguin Books Ltd., 80 Strand, London WC2R 0RL, England
Penguin Ireland, 25 St. Stephen's Green, Dublin 2,
Ireland (a division of Penguin Books Ltd.)
Penguin Group (Australia), 250 Camberwell Road, Camberwell, Victoria 3124,
Australia (a division of Pearson Australia Group Pty. Ltd.)
Penguin Books India Pvt. Ltd., 11 Community Centre, Panchsheel Park,
New Delhi - 110 017, India
Penguin Group (NZ), 67 Apollo Drive, Rosedale, North Shore 0632,
New Zealand (a division of Pearson New Zealand Ltd.)
Penguin Books (South Africa) (Pty.) Ltd., 24 Sturdee Avenue,
Rosebank, Johannesburg 2196, South Africa

Penguin Books Ltd., Registered Offices:
80 Strand, London WC2R 0RL, England

Published by New American Library, a division of Penguin Group (USA) Inc.
Previously published in a New American Library edition.

First New American Library Trade Paperback Printing, February 2009
10 9 8 7 6 5 4

 REGISTERED TRADEMARK—MARCA REGISTRADA

New American Library Trade Paperback ISBN: 978-0-451-22619-8

The Library of Congress has cataloged the hardcover edition of this title as follows:

McElwain, Jason.
    The game of my life : a true story of challenge, triumph, and growing up autistic/
Jason "J-Mac" McElwain with Daniel Paisner.
        p. cm.
    ISBN: 978-0-451-22301-2
1. McElwain, Jason—Health.   2. Autism—Patients—United States—Biography.
3. Basketball players—United States—Biography.   I. Paisner, Daniel.   II. Title.
RC553. A88M384 2008
616.85'8820092—dc22   2007032261
[B]

Set in Adobe Garamond
Designed by Ginger Legato

Printed in the United States of America

Never give up, never give in.
Be motivated in everything you do,
if you want to catch a dream.
The sky's the limit.
Give all that you can,
if you want to catch a dream.

—Jason McElwain
Original Rap Lyrics

CONTENTS

Contents

THE GAME OF MY LIFE

Pregame

JASON'S STORY

ON THE NIGHT OF FEBRUARY 15, 2006, in a high school gymnasium in a suburb of Rochester, New York, something remarkable happened: an autistic teenager named Jason McElwain took the court for the Greece Athena Trojans varsity basketball team. And he didn't just take it—he grabbed it with both hands and made it his own.

That he was there at all, in uniform, was remarkable, considering that until he was three years old Jason McElwain refused to eat unless he was forced to do so. He didn't speak until he was five. He spent most of his early childhood sitting beneath his parents' dining room table, banging together two packs of Trident Bubble Gum, or alone in the corner of his special-needs classroom, disconnected from the other children. As a child, he was unable to maintain eye contact or respond to the most basic external stimuli. His body went rigid at the slightest touch. He often appeared to stare blankly across the room. His parents worried that they would never reach him, that Jason would remain closed off from the simple social interactions that moved the rest of the world.

Young Jason was prone to autistic outbursts and erratic behavior that included rocking back and forth, flapping his arms, and humming in a low moan. And yet through Jason's fog of autism, he somehow formed a close bond with his brother, Josh. They would have been like twins, except for the profound differences in their personalities and affect, and yet over time, Jason's parents began to notice that Jason would mimic his brother and follow in his footsteps—almost literally—as he was learning to walk. The relationship ran counter to an article Jason's parents had read on autism, which suggested that autistic children might never experience such points of connection in a sibling relationship, while at the same time it seemed to confirm another article, which suggested that autistic children are often "raised" and primarily influenced by their healthy siblings.

Like many autistic children, Jason had his obsessive interests, and for the longest time he lived and breathed basketball. If he wasn't playing it, he was watching it, or thinking about it, or following the accounts of his NBA heroes in the newspaper or on ESPN's *SportsCenter*. He dribbled a ball, up and down the street, everywhere he went. He spent countless hours on his driveway court, playing knockout or H-O-R-S-E with Josh. Each Christmas, his mother would buy him a new basketball and say it was a present from Josh, and each Christmas Jason would tear the gift wrapping from his new basketball like he couldn't wait to see what was inside. He was never disappointed.

That this determined young man could overcome his various

disabilities to stand on a high school basketball court alongside some of the strongest players in the region was astonishing. But there was more to Jason's story than a token appearance in a single game. The game took place on Senior Night, the last regular-season game on the Trojans' schedule, and it was a long-standing tradition at Greece Athena to honor graduating players just before the game. Their parents were on hand, snapping photos. Their mothers received flowers. Seniors who didn't normally get a chance to start would find themselves in the starting lineup. Seniors who only played a little would play a little more. And a senior like Jason McElwain, who as team manager was charged with keeping his teammates focused during games and practices, would be allowed to dress in uniform as an honorary team member. It was a way to give something back to a kid who had given so much of himself to the team, who had missed out on so much as well.

Adding to the big deal was Coach Jim Johnson, who had taken Jason aside at the beginning of the season to promise him he would get to dress in uniform for the game. And if the moment presented itself, he said, he would get Jason into that final game. Underneath this goal, Coach Johnson made a wish: he hoped like hell his players would get Jason the ball for an open look and the kid would have a chance to score.

Jason McElwain was not physically disabled, but his development had been so substantially slowed by this disorder that to play in a meaningful high school basketball game was a pipe dream. He wasn't big enough, quick enough, or strong enough to play in a program that could probably fill out a junior college roster with its starters. The former Syracuse All-American and 1996 first-round NBA draft pick John Wallace was a Greece

Athena alum—his brother Rickey was on the 2004/05 and 2005/06 Trojans teams—so the caliber of ball ran high.

Alongside that pipe dream came another: the Greece Athena Trojans were battling for the Monroe County Division II championship. They were tied for second place with their rivals from Irondequoit High School, at 8 wins and 3 losses, one game behind division-leading Webster Thomas, at 9 and 2. To finish at the top of the standings was every coach's goal, every player's fantasy, every team manager's obsession, and here it was within reach. In the world of Monroe County high school basketball, this was as good as it gets, while in the narrow, fixated world of Jason McElwain, this was all that mattered.

And so the game meant something to the Trojans' graduating seniors and their families. It meant something to Coach Johnson and his returning players, who were determined to finish on top of the division standings, and to make a statement going into the postseason sectionals tournament that would cap the school season. It meant something to the Greece Athena community, which had long prided itself on its rich basketball tradition. And it meant the world to Jason McElwain. The chance to play. The chance at a division title. The chance at the sectionals. The chance to be like everyone else.

For the seventeen years leading up to this one night, Jason McElwain wasn't looking to stand out so much as to fit in. He was thinking big, but he wasn't thinking about winning championships. All he wanted, really, was to be in the running, to be going through the same motions as the other kids his age, to be a part of something that was bigger than himself. He could not articulate these things, but that didn't make them any less meaningful.

And yet what he couldn't say he could somehow accomplish. He had gotten past a childhood diagnosis of severe autism to where he could function at a moderate level. He could get himself to and from school, follow directions, interact appropriately with his teachers and peers, and focus on simple tasks at hand. He could let himself into an empty house at the end of his school day and complete a few simple chores before his mother came home from work. He could read at about the fourth-grade level. He wasn't "mainstreamed" in any kind of traditional sense, but he took gym and sometimes music with the other kids, beginning in elementary school. By his senior year of high school, he took shop and auto mechanics at Greece Athena as well.

Most important, he had friends. Sure, he was sometimes the object of various taunts and pranks. Once, a few of the players tried to stuff him into a gym locker, but that wasn't so bad, Jason said. Another time, they hid his jacket and some of his things, but the guys were just kidding around. On still another occasion, they encouraged him to hide beneath the bottom bench step of the gymnasium bleachers, so that they could close him up inside. They did this as a joke, with Jason happy to be included in the prank, but then they turned off the lights to the gym and allowed Jason to think he had been abandoned there, stuck in the folds of the wooden bleachers.

Gradually, Jason learned to distinguish the good-natured teasing from the cruelty and fit himself into the elaborate social network of Greece Athena High School. He went from being a tagalong kid whose constant presence was grudgingly accepted by his older brother's friends to someone able to pursue appropriate social relationships on his own. He went from being the butt of these school-yard jokes to being in on them. At the end of his senior year, he had over a hundred numbers stored in his cell phone directory—about a hundred more than his mother could have imagined.

Along the way, his interest in sports had continued. As a freshman, he went out for the cross-country team, with the stipulation that the coach would make sure there was someone to help him tie his shoes before practices and meets. As a five-foot six-inch sophomore, he tried out for the junior varsity basketball team, and when he didn't make the cut the coach asked him to stay on as team manager. His mother pushed hard for this. She actually called the coach and told him what it would mean. She didn't care that Jason wouldn't play in a single game. She just wanted him to feel a part of something that was important to him, to have something to look forward to at the end of each school day, to find an outlet for his obsession.

Jason thrived in this role. He took his job as team manager seriously. He dressed in shorts and sneakers for practice and wore a shirt and tie for games. He collected rebounds during free throw drills. He helped run the clock. He filled the team water bottles before each game, and passed out towels to players as they came off the court for a breather. He even got into a game. This was a surprise. It was the last game of the season, the junior varsity version of Senior Night. Coach Jeff Amoroso had handed him a uniform the night before. The coach had told Jason he would try to let him play, but Debbie McElwain warned her son not to get his hopes up. She hated to see him disappointed, but Coach Amoroso kept his word. With just under two minutes to go in the game and his team up 48–35 against Irondequoit, Jason McElwain crossed from the bench to the scorer's table. The Greece Athena gymnasium was starting to fill for the varsity game that would follow, and the crowd went a little crazy when Jason stepped onto the floor. He was such a joyful, animated, outgoing presence at games, cheering on his teammates, that he was impossible to miss. He was almost like the team mascot. Everybody wanted to see him do well.

A collection of thirty or so students sat in a special cheering section in the corner of the gym, beneath a banner marked "The 6th Man," and they led the crowd in a rhythmic chant: "J-Mac!" *Clap, clap.* "J-Mac!" *Clap, clap.* It was a nickname borrowed from Syracuse University's Gerry McNamara, who was known to die-hard college hoops fans throughout upstate New York as G-Mac. Coach Johnson pinned the name on Jason one afternoon at a summer basketball clinic. He figured if Syracuse could have a G-Mac, Greece could have a J-Mac. Soon Jason was calling himself J-Mac as well. He did this without the bluster of professional athletes, like Allen Iverson, who referred to themselves by their nicknames ("I am the Answer!"), but with the charm and innocence of a kid who was merely thrilled to have a nickname.

With about forty seconds left on the clock, Jason took the ball at the top of the key. He was the smallest kid on the court, his uniform about two sizes too big, and yet you looked on and just knew Jason would attempt a three. That's one of the things about autism. Those who suffer from it are typically fearless, and unable to anticipate any downside to any action, and that certainly described Jason McElwain on the basketball court. There was a swagger to his movement, a confidence that came from picturing himself in just this spot, over and over in his head. He was Gerry McNamara, Kobe Bryant, and John Wallace all rolled into one. A lot of kids, you put them out there in that kind of situation, they'd be too timid to take the ball to the basket or attempt an outside shot, but not Jason. He'd lived this moment in his driveway, so there was every reason to be confident. There was no downside. The first time he touched the ball, he dished it off to a teammate, but he followed his pass and called for the ball. As soon as he got it back, he fired up a three-point shot. It fell short of the rim, but the defender had brushed up against Jason as he was releasing the ball and was called for a foul.

Jason stepped to the line for the first of three free throws. The Greece Athena crowd was silent as Jason attempted his first foul shot. It was as if every player, every coach, every student, every parent . . . every *janitor* in that gymnasium was caught wishing the same thing: that Jason McElwain would somehow make a free throw. Just one. That's all anyone dared ask of this moment. Anyone, that is, except Josh McElwain, who firmly believed his brother would hit all three. Josh had seen Jason take enough free throws to know the kid was money on the line. Josh closed his eyes and imagined how the crowd might react if his brother sank three in a row. It could happen, he thought. It really, really could happen.

Here again, Jason McElwain was fearless, like he'd been shooting free throws in front of a crowd his entire life. He went into the routine he had practiced for as long as he could remember—on his driveway court, in the mirror, in his dreams. He spun the ball on the dribble. He bounced the ball a few times more. He drew a deep breath. He bent his knees, and allowed himself the slightest jump as he released the ball high. And then he rattled the rim and scored the first point of his high school basketball career.

People began banging on the bleachers. Jason stood at the line and guessed this was what thunder sounded like, up close. The 6th Man section resumed its rhythmic chant: "J-Mac!" *Clap, clap.* "J-Mac!" *Clap, clap.* All around the gym, people were smiling, cheering, clapping. Even the opposing players were caught up in it.

The referee passed the ball back to Jason, and once again the gym quieted. Once again, Jason stepped calmly to the free throw line, drew his deep breath, spun his dribble, bounced the ball, bent his knees, and shot. Once again, Jason sent the ball through the hoop. This time it was a clean swish. This time the cheering was louder still.

"J-Mac!" *Clap, clap.* "J-Mac!" *Clap, clap.*

He hit the third shot too, another swish, and now there was pandemonium in the Greece Athena stands. Anyway, it was as close to pandemonium as the crowd could muster. There were only about one hundred people in the stands, but they made noise like one thousand.

"J-Mac!" *Clap, clap.* "J-Mac!" *Clap, clap.*

The game had been out of reach when McElwain came in, but now it wasn't about the game. Now it was about Jason McElwain and the unlikely storybook ending he had written to the junior varsity season. And he wasn't done just yet. He meant to put an exclamation point on things, attempting a second three-pointer the next time down the court, but the ball hit the front of the rim as the final buzzer sounded. Still, it was a defining moment, and Jason would talk about this game every day for the next two years. He would think about it constantly. He would go over it in his mind, or with his father, or with his brother. He would eat the same pregame meal—ravioli, green beans, chicken noodle soup, and a cup of milk—before every varsity game the following season. He would watch the tape from that final junior varsity game. He would go through the same pregame routines. The memory of the game became more than a highlight reel, more than a proud moment. It was Jason's obsession for the game of basketball squared and turned inside out. It was Jason's sense of self, burned onto two minutes of VHS tape that he would now have to watch before every significant moment in his life.

It was life itself.

Autism is a developmental disorder that generally appears in childhood, typically in children under three years of age. The disorder is characterized by a marked impairment in social interaction (including but not limited to an aversion to being touched, avoidance of eye contact, and an inability to judge appropriate social behavior), and delayed development of communication skills, and is often accompanied by obsessive thinking and repetitive actions, such as tapping against a table.

Debbie and David McElwain had never even heard the term "autism" when Jason was diagnosed at age two and a half, but they did not question the diagnosis. In the backs of their minds, in the place where their worst fears went to hide, they expected as much. The symptoms matched their child almost as if they had been written specifically about Jason. Debbie had been convinced there was something wrong ever since Jason was a couple months old, but she and her husband had been torn between thinking something was *off* with Jason and that he was merely slow to develop. Now, at last, they had a name for what was different about Jason: autism.

Immediately, the McElwains set about reading as much as they could about the disorder so that they would be better posi tioned to advocate for Jason's care. Debbie especially became fairly expert in the treatments and facilities that were available at the time. There wasn't much, but she was determined to defy the doctors' prognoses and help her son to live an active, healthy, *involved* life. Anyway, she was determined to try.

There is no known cure for autism, Debbie McElwain learned, which means an individual cannot "grow out" of a childhood diagnosis of autism, although symptoms may lessen as a child develops, receives treatment, and learns to control socially inappropriate behavior. For reasons researchers have been unable to explain, the disorder is four times more prevalent in males than in females, and overall incidence of autism is consistent across all racial, ethnic, and social lines, meaning it can touch any family, anywhere, at any time. But Debbie cared only that the disorder had touched her family, at this time. The numbers and trends would not apply to Jason, she determined. The map they'd been handed would not be the map of their experience. Whatever it took, Debbie McElwain would help her son beat the long odds against him, in whatever ways she could. Together, they would become the exceptions to the unwritten rules.

By the end of Jason McElwain's final year at Greece Athena, he was a senior in name only. Privately, his parents worried he would never achieve his GED, even as he made plans to continue in his pursuit of same. Already, his teachers were saying a GED might be just out of reach, but it was something to strive for. Always, Debbie McElwain thought, Jason needed something to strive for.

In the meantime, he still had his basketball, and by now he had moved to the varsity, where he continued in his role as team manager. Coach Johnson was thrilled with Jason's extra efforts. The kid went to every team practice and worked hard to motivate his teammates. His mantra, "Stay focused," became a kind of rallying cry for the team, and during games Jason was the first off the bench to offer one of the players a towel or a high five. Like the junior varsity coach before him, Coach Johnson wanted to reward Jason with a chance to appear in a game, and he set about doing just that. He collected the last jersey from his pile and presented it to Jason the day before the final home game of the regular season. Earlier in the season, the jersey had belonged to a player named Ryan Novitski, who had left the team. If that jersey hadn't been lying around in his office, Coach Johnson would have had to make up a new one, because he was determined to dress Jason for the game. He had given Jason his word at the beginning of the season, but more than that he believed it was the right thing to do.

On January 18, 2006, when the Greece Athena Trojans visited the Spencerport Rangers, Johnson approached Spencerport coach Josh Harter. Coach Johnson had looked ahead on the schedule and saw that Greece Athena would be hosting Spencerport for the Senior Night game. He said, "I really want to honor this kid for our last home game and put him in uniform, but I don't want to do anything to embarrass your team."

Harter and his players knew J-Mac, and understood his role on the team. It's a small, close-knit community, the high school basketball community in and around Rochester. The two schools were like friendly rivals. Some of the players had been squaring off a couple times a season since middle school. A lot of Coach Harter's guys knew Jason from area camps and clinics, and from other school contests. They'd heard about that junior varsity game, when he hit those three free throws. Coach Harter said he would certainly be supportive of putting Jason out on the floor in the Senior Night game, and encouraged Johnson to pursue it. He would not give his players any special instructions, he said, only to treat Jason's presence on the court with respect.

Next, Coach Johnson approached the Greece Athena athletic director, Randy Hutto, who himself was the father of an autistic child. Johnson guessed Hutto would also be supportive of the plan, but he needed to clear it with him just the same. Hutto was extremely private about his own family among the Greece Athena faculty, but his situation was well known, and as Johnson hoped, he too endorsed the plan to try to get Jason into this final game.

When Senior Night rolled around on the calendar, Jason McElwain was pumped. His mother warned him all over again not to get his hopes up, but his hopes were already through the roof. Still, she tried to ground him. It was one thing to get into the final minute of a meaningless junior varsity game. It was quite another to get into a game with these big varsity players. Jason, at five feet ten, was a little taller than he had been just a couple years earlier, but he was still all skin and bones standing next to some of these kids, and the last thing Debbie McElwain wanted was to see him get hurt. The second-to-last thing she wanted was to see him disappointed. She didn't know whether to pray for him to get into the game or to keep his seat on the bench.

Finally, with 4:19 on the clock and a comfortable lead, Coach Johnson sent Jason to the scorer's table. The scene was like a repeat of his junior varsity appearance, only on a larger stage. The Greece Athena gym was packed. Word was out that Jason might get into the game, and folks turned out to cheer him on. Members of the Greece Athena faculty who didn't normally attend basketball games had turned out to support Jason and the team's graduating seniors. Prominent alums and community officials were on hand. Even John Wallace, the best basketball player to ever wear the black and gold of Greece Athena, was in the bleachers to watch his brother Rickey and his friends. The 6th Man cheering section was bigger, louder, and more energetic than Coach Johnson could remember. They had a bunch of gold T-shirts printed up, with "The 6th Man" emblazoned on the front. They started in with their standard cheer: "J-Mac!" *Clap, clap.* "J-Mac!" *Clap, clap.* It was the same rhythmic chant heard in high school gymnasiums across the country, only with Jason's nickname slotted at the front end. Also, there were a couple dozen pictures of Jason's head scattered around the 6th Man cheering section in the corner of the gym. They were affixed to paint-stirring sticks and being held up like masks. The effect was almost surreal, to see Jason stepping onto the court while all around another couple dozen floating Jason heads cheered him on. There were three or four different poses: Jason cheering, Jason smiling, Jason focusing on the game. The pictures had been the idea of Jay Shelofsky, a Greece Athena parent whose son had been a teammate of Jason's when he sank those three free throws. It was a way to acknowledge what Jason had meant to the Greece Athena basketball program, a way to put a kind of flourish on his high school career.

The story might have ended here, and for Jason and his family, it would have been enough, but what happened next was like something out of a Disney movie. Actually, it was like something out of a Disney movie that could never get made, because no one would believe the pitch. In just over four minutes, Jason

McElwain erupted for twenty points and tied what Coach Johnson believed was the school record for the most three-pointers in a game, with six. (No one kept school records for three-pointers prior to Coach Johnson's arrival, so at least it was a record for his program.) To put a fine point on things, Jason did his erupting in just over three minutes, because it took more than a minute for him to sink his first basket. He was just as fearless as he had been his first time on the court in a high school game, but his first couple shots wouldn't fall. Here again, it was the kind of rough start that might have discouraged a less determined young soul, but Jason McElwain kept on shooting. Here again, there was no downside.

In the end, it was a performance that amazed every last person in the Greece Athena gymnasium—including, quite frankly, Jason McElwain. About the only person who wasn't surprised by it was Jason's brother, who was away at college in Geneseo, New York, and unable to attend the game. He might have come, but there was a snowstorm in the forecast upstate, and he was unsure of the roads. Plus, Josh McElwain had spent so much time shooting hoops with his brother on their driveway court that he fully expected Jason to light it up, if he ever got the chance. He didn't need to be seated in the Greece Athena gym to cheer his brother on. Jason knew he had his brother's full support and enthusiasm, as well as the weight of his expectations. David McElwain called Josh on his cell phone right after the game to tell him what had just happened, how his brother had just scored twenty points to highlight the Senior Night game, and Josh had to keep himself from shrugging his shoulders. He was thrilled, but he was not surprised.

And yet it was an autistic outburst no one could have imagined.

No one who was in that gymnasium could quite believe the way Jason kept draining three-pointer after three-pointer. Yes, it was probably true that in a show of sportsmanship the Spencerport Rangers were not guarding Jason as closely as they might have, but Jason still had to make all those baskets. Six three-pointers! And his lone two-point field goal might as well have been another long-range bomb, because his foot was on the three-point line.

"I was as hot as a pistol," Jason said later, repeating a line he had heard to describe his game and that would now be featured in almost every interview he would give in its wake.

Debbie McElwain raced down to the court to find her son after the game. He was being carried around on the shoulders of his teammates, accepting the high fives and congratulations of more students than she could count. She looked on and tried to imagine the rigid, aloof little boy who would not be touched alongside the jubilant young man on the receiving end of all this attention. She pushed her way through the crowd to get to Jason, and when she finally reached him she cupped his face between the palms of her hands the way she used to do when he was a child. Around her, there were those couple dozen pictures of Jason, bouncing up and down among the joyful crowd, but she tried to block them out. She held the real Jason as tight as she could, as close as she could, for as long as she could. "Don't you cry," she said to him firmly. "Don't you dare cry."

It was as much a caution to herself as it was a reminder to Jason. But Jason didn't need reminding. He wasn't about to cry. He was too busy strutting around the gym like a conquering hero, posing for pictures with the pretty young cheerleaders, signing autographs, soaking in the moment as if its memory would have to last a long, long time.

What follows is the remarkable story of a remarkable young man, his remarkable family, and his remarkable coaches and teammates—told, as much as possible, by Jason McElwain himself. That qualifier, *as much as possible*, is key. To some, the notion of an autistic teenager narrating his own story might seem like a literary conceit, but there is nothing artificial about Jason's ability to share his experiences. Despite his autism, Jason can clearly recall events and circumstances in postadolescence, even though he has almost no firsthand childhood memories beyond the warehousing of stories that have been told and retold among friends and family. Certainly, there are holes in his memory, but so are there holes in the memories of our leading memoirists and autobiographers. Such is the selective nature of the human mind. Regarding his early childhood, Jason remembers what has been passed down to him, just, but he is perfectly capable of placing an incident in context and turning over the storytelling for a paragraph or two to someone better positioned to tell the tale. In this way, those with more insight on an aspect of Jason's story will be allowed to weigh in, as in an oral history.

"I don't really pay attention to all that autism stuff," Jason notes. "I just think of myself as normal, like everybody else. Something happens to me, it can make me happy or sad, depending on what it is. A lot of that stuff that happened a long time ago, I can remember that it happened, even though I don't really remember it happening. And it's not because of autism that I don't remember. A lot of my friends don't remember stuff that happened to them back in grade school. They don't remember what they had for dinner. But I've heard these stories so many times, so that's why I remember them. And this last basketball season, I remember everything. That night in the gym. My final game. Me scoring all those points. Us winning the division and going on to the sectionals. It's like it's still happening."

Yes, it *is* like it's still happening, and this book is like an extension of that one special night. Yes, Jason McElwain's memory is alive with detail and emotion. He has a way with words that is raw and pure and utterly refreshing, and a kind of unvarnished insight that seems entirely his own. Read on and see if you don't agree.

—Daniel Paisner
October 2007

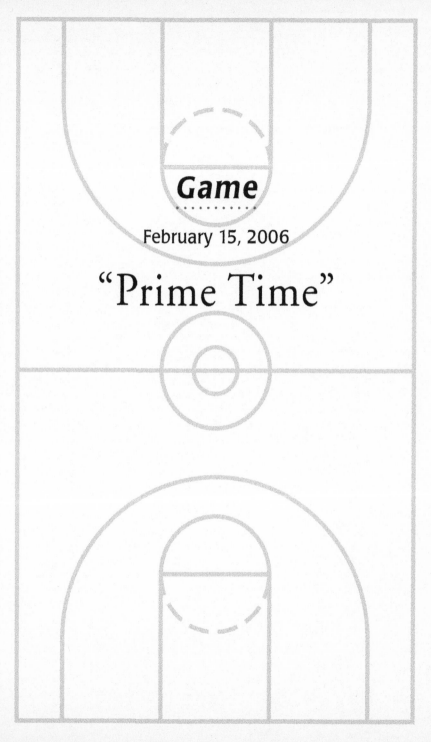

Game

February 15, 2006

"Prime Time"

SENIOR NIGHT WAS PRETTY IMPORTANT. I was looking forward to it like you wouldn't believe. My mom
was trying to get me to think it wasn't so important,
but you can't change how important something is just
by pretending it isn't. You can't just say it's a regular game. Come
on, it's like one of the biggest nights of the high school basketball
season. At Greece Athena, where I went to school, everybody
comes out for it. It's like a tribute. It's when you say good-bye to
all the seniors on the team, when they get congratulated for all
the hard work they've put in. A lot of the teachers are there, and
the principal, people like that. A lot of the students. The gym
can get really packed, and for the seniors on the team, it's like the
highlight of the season. They look forward to it their whole ca-
reers, because they treat you like a celebrity. You're announced over
the public-address system before the game, people cheer for you,
and then your parents meet you at half court and you pose for
pictures. You give your mother flowers. It's a whole big ceremony.

I used to go to the Senior Night games and think what it would be like to be one of the graduating players, to be on the court with my parents when they said my name and everyone cheered. When Coach Johnson told me I would be in uniform for this last game, this was what I thought about. He didn't say at first it was Senior Night, but I knew. I knew our schedule by heart. He said it was the last home game of the season, so of course it was Senior Night. After that he said yes, it was also going to be Senior Night. He said I would be announced over the public-address system just like everyone else. He said I was a member of the team and I should hear my name called out in front of the whole gym, just like everyone else. It was to show everyone how much I contributed to the team the past two seasons, because I had also been the team manager during my junior year. He didn't promise me I would get to play, but he did say I would be in this special ceremony, and I remember being really happy about that, really excited. Obviously, I wanted to play, and I was hoping I would get into the game, but the special ceremony was also cool. That was like a bonus. I remember thinking it would be nice for my mom and dad to be down on the court like that, being announced in front of everybody, and me giving my mom flowers and everything. I didn't usually give her flowers, and I thought she would probably like them.

I had been working with the team all season, helping Coach Johnson during practice, helping the players during the games, trying to keep everyone focused and motivated. That was always my big thing, for everyone to stay focused. It didn't matter if we were up by ten or down by ten, you had to keep your head in the game. That's basketball. You can't lose your focus. Every possession, every time down the court, you had to be focused. On defense, too. You couldn't let up. So I would shout it out, over and over: "Stay focused! Stay focused!" You heard those words, you knew they were coming from me. That was like my big contribution. I said it so many times that soon the other guys started saying it, too. It caught on.

I remember bringing home my uniform the night before the game. It was a Tuesday night. I carried it in a plastic bag. I showed it to my mother and she was like, *Aw, Jason, that's great, but don't get your hopes up.* She didn't say anything but I knew what she was thinking. She knew I really wanted to play, and she didn't want me to be disappointed if I didn't. She was always protecting me from being disappointed, but I was like, *Let's just go to the game and see what happens.* I knew Coach would get me in, so I wasn't too worried about it. If he did, he did. If he didn't, he didn't. Anyway, I wanted my mom to see the uniform. That's all. It was number 52. It wasn't my lucky number or anything. It was just a number. Coach said it was the last one he had so I didn't get to choose. When my dad came home, I showed it to him, too. He smiled when I showed it to him, this really big smile he has that I really like. I think he probably thought I'd get into the game, too. He was like me, he wasn't too worried about it. Plus, I think he wanted it to happen almost as much as I wanted it to happen.

That whole night, I kept looking at my uniform. I was just looking at it and looking at it. I couldn't believe I had my own varsity basketball uniform. All my life, this was what I wanted. It was like a dream come true. I tried it on, and after that I didn't want to take it off. I liked how it looked on me. I liked how it felt. Like I'd been wearing one my whole career. Sometimes, before a big game, a lot of the guys would wear their jerseys to school. It was a way to get everyone excited about the game, like a school spirit thing. I thought about if I should wear my jersey to school the next day. Then I thought about going outside and shooting some hoops in my driveway, but I decided not to because I didn't want to get my uniform dirty. Then I took it off and had dinner.

That whole next day in school, people kept coming up to me and wishing me luck. Most times, before a big game, people would wish me luck because they knew I was the team manager. My teachers and everyone, the other kids, they knew I was part of the team. But this time it was different. This time I would be on the court with everyone else. Wearing a uniform. Sitting on the bench. Maybe getting into the game. This time I would be like a regular player, not just the team manager. So it was the same, everyone wishing me luck like that, but it was also different. There was a lot of excitement about it, not just from me but from the whole school. Everyone was talking about the game. It was like there was nothing else going on.

I couldn't wait for the game to start. Ask anyone who knows me, ask my mom or dad or my brother, and they'll tell you I have a hard time waiting. I'm not so patient. When something's coming, when something's about to happen, I want it to just hurry up and happen. I'm like, *Enough already! Let's go!* I guess a lot of people are the same way, but on other people you don't notice it. On me, you notice it. I think probably this is because of my autism. I think it makes me not so patient. That's what my doctor always said. Dr. Vora. He said I needed to learn how to relax and be patient, because if you tell me you'll look into something, I'll ask you about it every day until you look into it and tell me what's happening about it. I get all nervous and jumpy and I start pacing back and forth. I start talking a lot and asking a lot of questions. I don't know what to do with myself; that's the expression people say for how nervous I can be, how jumpy. When I was little, I used to wave my arms back and forth whenever I got excited, almost like I was flapping, but I didn't do that anymore. At first I had to keep my hands in my pockets to keep from doing it, but after that I just stopped doing it.

The junior varsity game before our game, it's like it took forever. That's how they do it in our high school. Before our game, our junior varsity team plays the junior varsity team of our opponent. That way both visiting teams can ride the same bus. We had to wait for them to finish, because we played back-to-back. When they were done and when they cleared the court, we could start with our Senior Night ceremony and then do our shoot-around, so I was really hoping it would be finished soon. I was talking and pacing and asking questions. I wanted to tell the kid who was keeping the clock to just let it run, because our game couldn't start until the junior varsity game was over. You can do that, you know, take a couple seconds off the clock just after they blow the whistle. Each time they blow the whistle, you can let it run another second or two until you stop it. I thought even just a couple seconds would help—that's how hard it was for me to wait. That's how excited I was.

Coach Johnson wasn't so patient either. Or he didn't like that we weren't so patient, because I wasn't the only one anxious for the Senior Night ceremony to start. I wasn't the only one pacing around. A lot of the players were jumpy and anxious. He told us to go just outside the door to the gym to wait for the junior varsity game to finish, and so we all stood by the door, like he told us. A few of the guys, they came over and said how good the uniform looked on me, how cool it was to see me suited up with the rest of the team. They congratulated me, and said they were happy for me, things like that. We pumped fists. This was what we did, just like the players we watched on television. High fives, handshakes . . . that was old school. I still liked to high-five, but the rest of the guys on the team, they would pump fists. It didn't matter to me either way. We were all getting excited, getting ready. A whole bunch of times, I'd seen these guys wait for big games to start, and now I was standing where they were standing, dressed how they were dressed, waiting how they were waiting, pumping fists like they were pumping fists. I'd always felt like a member of the team when I was just the team manager, but now I really felt like a member of the team. I was just like everyone else.

It wasn't just because it was Senior Night that this was a big game. No, it was a big game all by itself. It was our last chance to win the division. We'd already earned a bye in the first round of the sectional tournament, which meant we didn't have to play until the second round, which was the quarterfinal round, but we all wanted to win, the division, too. That was what we'd worked so hard for, all season long. What would have to happen was we would have to win, and Webster Thomas, which was a game ahead of us, they would have to lose. There was also another team, Irondequoit, and they were tied with us, but it didn't matter if they won or lost. It mattered to them, I'm sure, but it didn't matter to us. If they won, and we won, and Webster Thomas lost, there would be a three-way tie for first place. If Irondequoit lost, and we won, and Webster Thomas lost, there would be a two-way tie. Either way, we had to win, and then hope for Webster Thomas to lose. Their game was going on at the same time as ours, so it's not like we could go and root against them or anything. It's not like we could keep track of the score. All we could do was take care of Spencerport, and to be honest, I wasn't too worried about Spencerport. We'd already beaten them earlier in the season, and we usually matched up pretty good against them.

I put on a white headband before the game. A lot of my friends wore headbands. Also, a lot of my favorite NBA players wore headbands. I liked the way it looked, so I put one on. My mom thought it made me look ridiculous, that was the word she used, but I thought it made me look like a basketball player. She said, "Jason, take that thing off." But I didn't think I looked ridiculous. I could see my reflection in the glass, looking in through the door to the gym, and there was J-Mac looking back at me. I almost didn't recognize myself. Number 52. Looking like everyone else on the team. Looking like a real basketball player. So I left it on.

The people were halfway into the gym when they started with the ceremony. Our games usually started on time, but this Senior Night ceremony could go on and on, so I guess some people took their time getting to the gym. Already, we were late getting started, and people were still coming in when they began calling out our names. They called us in one at a time. They called us in and said our names and the people would cheer. Then we'd walk past our bench and shake Coach's hand and then meet our parents at half court and walk across the court through a kind of arch they'd set up, with yellow and black balloons. Those were our school colors, yellow and black. When you were in the arch, you were supposed to stop and pose for pictures. I watched the first couple players whose names were called, so I would know what to do. This took a few minutes, because they took a lot of pictures. There were seven seniors, including me, so all these minutes, all these pictures, they added up.

I went just after my friend Steve Kerr. Steve usually wore number 25, but tonight he was planning to wear number 4. He told me about it when we were outside in the hall, waiting to be called in. The reason for this was there was another senior, Matt Sheehan, and he usually wore number 4. The thing about Matt was he never really had a chance to start, and he was supposed to start this game against Spencerport, but he hurt himself that day in gym class and now he couldn't play, so Steve got the idea to wear Matt's number. The guys on the team were all sad for Matt, especially because he got hurt that very day and he had been all pumped to finally get a chance to start that night, and then Steve came up with this plan. It would be like Matt was starting—that's how he put it. Like however many points Steve scored wearing number 4, he'd be scoring for Matt. Everyone thought this was a great idea. I thought so, too. Steve was one of our starters, so it didn't mean the same thing to him as it would have meant to Matt, starting this final game or scoring all those points for himself. Anyway, they called Matt's name for Senior Night, and he came out on crutches, wearing his regular jersey, and after that, he gave the jersey to Steve, and it got a big applause when they did this. Everyone understood what it meant.

When my turn came, I walked past Coach and shook his hand. My parents were waiting for me at half court. They were smiling these really big smiles. I gave my mother her flowers, and then we turned and walked across the court through the arch. I walked in between. My dad is really tall, and my mom is really short, and I stood in the middle as we posed for pictures. We were in size order. It just worked out like that. Someone told me later we looked like we were tilted, and that the photographer must have had a hard time getting all of us into the picture, with my dad being so tall and my mom being so short and me being in the middle. I thought that was pretty funny. It cracked me up.

After all the seniors were called, Coach joined us on the court and we took a bunch of team pictures. First we took pictures with just the team, and then we took pictures with the parents. There was a regular photographer taking pictures for the school, and a lot of people had their own cameras and they were taking pictures, too. Some of the players were taking their own pictures. This went on for a while, and I was ready to burst, that's how anxious I was for the game to start. And if I was on Spencerport, man, I would have been really ready to burst, because this wasn't even my school and there was all this celebrating going on, all these people posing for pictures, holding up the game. The Spencerport players weren't taking any pictures. They were just waiting.

Finally, Coach Johnson cleared the court and we began our pregame shootaround. This was cool. This was what I was waiting for, to be out there taking my layups and my jumpers, getting ready. People were still coming into the gym, and I'd look up and see my friends or someone I knew, and I'd wave hello. I was trying to focus on the game, trying to get ready, but it was hard because a lot of people wanted to congratulate me or wish me good luck or just say hello. It was hard because I'd never been down there on the floor before, warming up. So I was back and forth between warming up and trying to concentrate and saying hello to everybody. There were even some players on the Spencerport team who came over to say something. I knew them because we'd played these guys a bunch of times. When I was on the junior varsity, some of these guys were on Spencerport's junior varsity, so we all kind of knew each other. They were good guys. I knew the coach, too, and he also came over to say hello and wish me luck.

There was music playing over the public-address system, and that also made it hard to concentrate. For all those games, all those shootarounds over the past couple seasons, I never realized how many distractions there were before a game. It's like I blocked them out. I was always busy lining up our water bottles or making sure our players' names and numbers were entered in the score book, so I never really noticed all the other stuff that goes on. But, man, there's a lot of other stuff going on, and when all you have to do is shoot it's hard to block it all out.

Eventually, though, the other stuff stopped and everyone stood for the national anthem and then it was time for the game to begin. The other seniors stepped out on the court for the opening tip-off. I was a senior, but I wasn't going to start. Coach told me this when he gave me the uniform, and he reminded me just before the game. But he didn't have to remind me. I knew. This was a big game for us, and he needed to go with our more experienced players to start. I just hoped we'd get out to a big lead and then maybe he could think about getting me in, so I took my seat on the bench and started cheering like crazy.

One

STAY FOCUSED

I'M USED TO PEOPLE LOOKING at me like I'm different. It doesn't bother me. I don't even notice it. When they ask me what it's like to be autistic, I don't know how to answer. It's just how I am. It's like asking someone what it's like to be tall or short, or fat or skinny. It's like asking a tomato what it's like to be a tomato. It's normal. It's me. I don't think I'm any different from anyone else. Really, I don't. I look at the world the same way as anyone else. I see myself in the mirror and how I look to other people. I think about things probably the same way you think about things. It's just that the world looks back at me a little funny, like I'm a little different. But like I said, I don't really notice it. I'm aware of it, but I try not to think about it because there's too much to do without thinking all the time what other people are thinking.

It's true that sometimes it's hard to put into words what's bouncing around in my head, but I know a lot of people who don't have autism who have the same problem. They say things they don't mean or mean things they don't say. They say one thing and do something else. They forget something they should probably remember. Chances are you probably know someone like that, too, someone who worries a little too much about how they look or act in a certain situation. But I've learned not to worry so much. I just do the best I can, whatever I'm doing. I try to be myself. That's all you can do, right? That's something I learned from my parents, and from my brother, Josh. Just keep going, you know. Be yourself. Stay focused. That's one of my big things, staying focused. If I have trouble getting my point across, if I can't control my emotions or my behavior, I take a deep breath and find my focus and start in again. I don't know where I got this from, but if I fall into one of my bad habits, like humming or flapping my hands or a whole bunch of different things I do when I don't even know I'm doing them, then someone just points it out to me and I focus on it and I get it under control. Usually it's my mom pointing it out to me, what I'm doing wrong, but I guess this is how it is for a lot of people, right? I guess my mom is like a lot of moms. She wants what's best for me. She wants everyone to see me in the best possible way. She doesn't want me to say or do anything to embarrass myself, but I don't really get embarrassed. I don't really care about that stuff. I went to a doctor once and he told me that autistic kids usually don't think about how they look to everyone else, and I think that's probably true about me. It's not true about my mom, though. She wants people to think I'm normal, but she's just looking out for me, the same way she looks out for my brother, Josh, and he's not autistic. He's away at college, and she still calls him every night to make sure he's eating properly, or cleaning his room, or doing his homework. She wants what's best for him, too.

I don't know if you've ever tried to focus really, really hard on something in order to make it happen, but it works. It's like a great trick. It doesn't have to be about an autistic outburst, or a particular type of behavior. It can be about anything. Just isolate on it and concentrate and you can control it. That's what focus can do. Anyway, that's what it does for me. All the time, whenever we had a big game, I kept telling all the guys on the team to keep their focus. That was like my theme. Over and over, I'd say this. The guys on the team would tease me about it. Coach said I was like a broken record. I didn't know what a broken record was, and someone had to explain it to me, and then I understood. But he was right. I can be like a broken record. That's how I'm able to focus, to concentrate. I repeat things to myself, over and over, until it comes. I just repeat myself and repeat myself and eventually I get it right. That's how I break things down. That's how I learn.

JIM JOHNSON (varsity basketball coach, Greece Athena Trojans)

This keeping focused became like a rallying cry for Jason. For the whole team, really. And he got more and more intense about it as we went into our postseason. You have to realize, after that final game, after he scored all those points, the media was all over him. He was a real celebrity. There were news cameras at all of our playoff games. One of the local sports guys was interviewing me before the McQuaid game, the sectionals semifinal, and when we were through, he asked if he could talk to Jason.

I was on the court at the time. Jason was up in the stands. So I called out to him. I said, "J-Mac, they want to interview you." He said, "Coach, no interviews now. I'm focused." It came out sounding almost funny, but he was serious. He was completely focused. Nothing was more important to this kid than winning that playoff game against McQuaid. It's like he was in some kind of zone.

Writing, too, is a good way for me to get my thoughts down so they make sense. It's a good way to focus, to break things down. Sometimes I wish I could write things out before I have to say them. Just having a regular conversation with someone, it would be so much easier if I had time to slow things down and think about how something will sound before I have to say it, because when I write it's much easier to communicate, to make sure I'm saying what I mean to say. But you don't have time to slow things down because the other people in the conversation are waiting for you to say your part of the conversation. It's your turn, and you have to go before they get tired of waiting. I don't know how it is for other people, but the world makes so much sense when everything is just in my head. It's when I have to put it out there that I get into trouble, so writing gives me time to think about what I'm saying and hear it back. It lets me organize my thoughts and make sure they come out right. I put it down and then I read it back and see if I sound like a normal kid. That's how I sound inside my head, like a normal kid, and that's how I want to sound to everyone else. For this book, the way I'm doing it is I'm speaking my thoughts into a tape recorder, and then when I get out everything I want to say, I read it back on paper and see how it is. Then I read it again and fix it up. Maybe I'll think of some more things I want to say, so I'll say them, too. Maybe there'll be some things I forgot, and some things I didn't remember right. And maybe I'll change my mind about something I wanted to say at first. I'm not actually holding a pencil in my hand or sitting in front of a computer, but it's a kind of writing. For me, it's the same thing as writing. It's organizing my thoughts and getting them down on paper in a way that tells what I'm thinking, what I remember, what I want to say about some of the incredible things that have happened to me. This is just how I have to do it, because there are too many pages and too many things that happened for me to write about everything in a regular way.

It's like when I give a speech. I'd never given a speech before that Senior Night game, and now all of a sudden, I give speeches all the time. I don't know, for some reason people want to hear me talk about basketball and trying hard and staying focused and holding on to your dreams. They never wanted to hear me talk about these things before, but they do now. Probably it's hard for my parents to picture me giving a speech, even now after they've seen me give a whole bunch of them, because they remember when I didn't talk. They remember when there was no one around to listen. They remember when I was just sitting by myself in the corner of a classroom, not playing with any of the other kids. So the idea of me giving a speech must be hard for them to believe. It's usually the same speech, and my parents helped me with it the first couple times, and after that, I had some other people help me, and then after a while I knew it pretty good. After a while, it felt like I'd been giving speeches my whole life. Also, I learned that if I don't prepare what I want to say ahead of time, if I don't make notes, it's easy to get lost. I panic a little bit. I lose my place. Like a lot of people, I guess. But if I have something written down beforehand, if I have a chance to look it over and try to memorize what I want to say and think about what kinds of questions people might ask, I'll usually do fine. It's like putting a little voice in your head to tell you what to do. Sometimes that voice is my mom's voice. Sometimes it's Coach Johnson's. Sometimes it's my dad's, or my brother's. Sometimes it's mine. But it helps to have a voice in there, telling you what to do. It helps you keep your place.

A lot of people, when they hear I'm writing a book, they look at me like I'm making a joke. They don't believe me. They think because I'm autistic I must be slow, or simple, or retarded. Well, I am slow. That's just how my brain works. It takes me a while to get the words out. It takes me a while to get them in, too. And it takes me a while to think about things in a way that I can understand them. Like I said, there are a lot of pages and a lot of stories to tell, and I have to do it in a special way and all of this takes a while. I'm simple, too. Not in a bad way, I don't think, but I like things a certain way. I like my routines, to break things down into patterns I can understand and control. Keep it simple—that's my thing. Like before a game, I'd have to go out and hit a three-pointer, then a double-pump layup, then a free throw. I was just the team manager, I wasn't dressed to play, but this was my pre-game drill down there on the court. I didn't participate in the team shootaround, but when everyone was done and it was my job to collect all the balls and put them away, I'd stop and take these few shots. I don't know if anyone else even noticed. Then

I'd run to center court and kiss the back of my ring finger and run back to the locker room to be with my teammates. Or that other routine, how I had to have the same pregame meal after I hit those three free throws in the junior varsity game I played my sophomore year: ravioli, green beans, chicken noodle soup, and a cup of milk. My mom had to buy a lot of that stuff during basketball season, because there were a lot of games.

Every game, this was what I had to do. It was all about routines for me, all the time. In basketball, and in everything else. And do you know what? Until that last game at the gym at my high school, I never changed that routine. Not just my pregame routine, but any of my routines. I'd hardly even left Rochester. But then everything got all exciting, and people started calling, and I started getting invited to all these places. All of a sudden, everything was different. So I had to figure out if I could change my routines and try to do all these other things, all at the same time. I had to give up some of that control, and it got really, really hard to keep things simple, the way I liked them. For a while, I didn't think I could do it, but I practiced. I kept my focus. I kept repeating to myself, over and over, whatever I had to do, running it through my head, over and over. It was important to me, so I worked at it. I had to think through what it would be like to sleep in a strange bed, in a strange hotel room, or to try different foods or be around new people. I don't think I'd ever been out of Rochester other than a couple trips to Disney World and one time to Connecticut for a special treatment and one other time to Washington, D.C. Now I've been to so many different places and on so many different planes I can't keep count, so for a long time that's what I focused on. I had to think what it would be like to give up the comfort of my routines, of what I knew. And it was more than that. It was thinking if I could talk onstage, or in front of a television camera, or in a roomful of strangers. If I had to give a speech or an interview, I'd have to sit with my mom or dad and work out what I wanted to say. I wasn't used to being the center of so much attention. Around my friends, around my school, I liked it when people talked to me and called out to me. I liked it when I was involved, so I guess you could say I didn't really mind being the center of attention. But that was in a place I knew, around people I knew. This was different. I wasn't used to being the center of this kind of attention. I didn't mind it, but I wasn't used to it, and writing all this stuff out beforehand really helped. It helped a lot.

My friends will tell you I liked being the center of attention, but that was with my friends. That was in school. I liked it that people were coming up to me, and pumping fists, and congratulating me. I liked it that I could make people laugh and feel good and smile. I liked posing for pictures with the other kids in my class, and some of the little kids I'd see around town. I liked signing autographs, which believe it or not a lot of people started asking me to do. That was pretty weird, like I was a celebrity, only I wasn't really a celebrity. I was still just J-Mac. I liked hearing from my friends' parents that they were happy for me, for what I'd done on the court. All of this, it was all right. It made me feel good. But by then this was part of my routine. By then the people around Greece already knew me as J-Mac. Even the other players, the other coaches, we'd play them twice each year, and after the first few times, they knew me. I'd go over to talk to them before the game. I wasn't shy. I used to be shy when I was little. I used to sit by myself and stare off into space. But now I'd talk to everybody. They'd tease me about how loud I was during the game, how enthusiastic. I didn't mind the teasing because it wasn't the mean kind of teasing. They knew I was really into the game, that I was really trying to pump up my team, that I was keeping my focus the only way I knew how.

But then I scored all those points on Senior Night, and everything changed. Then I was the center of attention in a way that wasn't too familiar. It was good and it was bad, all at the same time. I was talking to people I didn't know, going to places I'd never been before. It was exciting, but it was also a little scary and confusing. All these things that were happening in school with people I knew, like posing for pictures and signing autographs, they now started happening outside of school, with people I'd never met. I didn't like that so much, until some people gave me some good advice. They said that meeting all these new people and experiencing all these new things was no different from meeting all those old people and experiencing all those familiar things for the first time. It's just that I'd taken the time to get comfortable with those people and things, and now I had to take the time to get comfortable all over again. That's all. Also, they said it was like all those baskets I used to shoot, on my hoop at home, with my brother, Josh. All the best players, the best shooters, they take a thousand shots a day. A thousand shots from the free throw line. A thousand shots from the corner. A thousand shots from the top of the key. A thousand layups. I don't think I took that many shots, but I took a lot of shots. After a while, it's like your memory. It becomes natural. Your body knows what to do because it's done the same thing so many times. That's how it is when you're autistic. Anyway, that's how it is for me.

BRIAN BENSON (childhood friend, Greece Athena teammate)

You should have seen Jason on the court, before one of our games. Not that final Senior Night game, but just a regular game. He knew everyone in the gym, it seemed. You'd look up, and he'd be in the stands, talking to some kid from the other school. Or he'd be talking to the other coach during warm-ups. I didn't know too many other kids like that. I certainly wasn't like that. But there was Jason, talking it up with the other coach.

Everybody knew Jason. Coach Johnson might not remember this, but he knew Jason long before Jason got to Greece Athena. Coach used to run these basketball camps, and Jason and I used to go to these camps together when we were ten or twelve years old. We did a lot of stuff like that together, when we were kids. And Jason stood out. It was hard not to notice him. People are just drawn to him. That's when Coach started calling him J-Mac, I think. All the way back then. And it was because Jason was just a real presence at those camps, a real personality. He worked hard at the basketball part, but he also worked hard at making people laugh, and making them notice him. And they did. In a good way, they did.

Some people say a team sport like basketball is not the best thing for an autistic kid, but basketball can be a team sport and an individual sport. It's both. A lot of people don't think about it in this way, but it's true. I've thought about this a lot. Think about it and maybe you'll see it's true. Why? It's because basketball is something you can do on your own, taking all those shots from all those different spots on the court. Over and over. It's like putting that voice inside your head, and repeating it, and practicing it until you're comfortable. Until you feel like you can control it. To me, it's the perfect sport for someone who's autistic, because there are all these drills you can do by yourself. You can shoot hoops in your backyard all day long. You can practice your dribble. Whatever you want to work on, you can just work on it and work on it and feel like you have some control over it. And then, when you do finally have some control over it, you can be a part of a team and work together to reach your goal. You can turn it into a social thing, and it can force you to meet new people and make friends with them and break some of the bad habits you might have gotten on your own.

Here's one other thing I want to talk about in this chapter, because it's also about staying focused. All the time, after a big game like the Super Bowl or the NBA playoffs, you'll see one of the players being interviewed and he'll say he was only trying to stay within himself. I watch a lot of sports, and you hear a lot of coaches say that, to stay within yourself, and a lot of players don't always know what they mean. Some of my friends on the team, if Coach Johnson told them to stay within themselves, they wouldn't know what he was talking about. But I think it means to do the best you can, to not worry so much about your opponent and worry only about what you can do to help your team win. If you try to do too much, you can get yourself in trouble, so don't try to do too much. Just do the best you can. That's what it means, I think. It's no different from the kinds of things my parents and my brother have been telling me my whole life, except here it's only about sports and with them it's about sports and everything else. Stay within yourself. Keep focused. Do the best you can. And don't worry about things you can't control.

I usually know what I want to say, but I can't always find the words, so I have to practice, and writing is like practice. I'm talking about writing the way I'm writing this book. Talking about something over and over and then reading it back and fixing it up and making it just right. This kind of writing is one way I can stay within myself. This kind of writing is trying to keep focused. This kind of writing is doing the best I can, and keeping control. And you know what else? This kind of writing is like basketball. It's like shooting all those hoops in my backyard. It lets me try on the words and see if they fit. Sometimes I can't find the words at all, and other times I just can't find them quick enough. And then there are other times when someone might help me find the word I'm looking for and I just agree to it. Like I said, I'm slow. And simple. But I'm not retarded. That's the one thing people always think when they hear the word "autism," they think it means you're retarded. Well, that's not true. Sometimes it makes me mad that people think that way, but mostly it makes me frustrated, the way people can treat you like you're not even there. They talk about you right in front of you, like you can't understand what they're saying. They don't take you seriously. It's frustrating—it really is.

LEVAR GOFF (high school friend, Greece Athena teammate)

We got to be pretty close, me and Jason, and I think one of the reasons was because I have an older brother with cerebral palsy. I grew up around kids who were a little different, and Jason was a little different. The other kids would tease him all the time, only it wasn't always positive. Some of it was mean, I thought. But Jason didn't know. They were taking advantage of him, but he just liked that they were paying attention to him. He just wanted to be accepted, and to joke around, just like everyone else.

One of the things we used to do together was make up little dumb songs. We'd be at his house, just making up songs, rapping and stuff. We'd get a rap going and he'd jump in and say his little rhyme. He loves to rap, Jason. He had a whole routine he used to do before every game, this original rap he wrote to get everyone motivated. He had to do his rap, and he'd go into it, and it was important to him, and sometimes people would hear it and start to laugh. Not the kids on the team—they knew Jason; they liked Jason—but the kids in the stands, they could hear. Sometimes, we'd have to tell him to stop, right in the middle of his rap, because these other kids would be making fun of him. Jason just thought they were laughing, and didn't really realize they were laughing at him. He wouldn't even have an idea. So he would just start

> laughing along with them, because with Jason, he just
> wanted to fit in. So bad, you know. That's really all he
> ever wanted, was to fit in.

Like I said, it's frustrating trying to get past what people think about you. I didn't mind so much, that people were making fun of me. It didn't happen a lot, and I didn't notice it a lot of the time. Sometimes, my friends would have to point it out. They'd tell me so-and-so wasn't really a good person because he was teasing me behind my back. Or my brother would tell me what was going on. And sometimes I'd notice it by myself, only I would pretend not to notice it, because it was easier that way. It was easier to just be myself and look the other way than to face up to it. My parents weren't good people to ask about this, because my father didn't pay good attention to this kind of stuff and my mother always thought all the kids were goofing on me. She thought it was like a hazing thing. She thought they were being cruel, when really they were just being kids. I didn't mind it so much. Like I said, it didn't happen all the time.

A lot of people, they don't really understand about autism. They hear the word and think it's like something they saw in a movie. I want to tell people that there are a lot of very successful people who have some type of autism. It's pretty common. Some people have a very severe form of it, and some people have a very mild form of it, and if you're on the mild side you can go to college and get a good job and live what a lot of people would call a normal life. I'm somewhere in between. With me, I started out having a very severe form of it; that's what the doctors told my parents when I was little. But then as I got older, I got more and more social, and I got involved in more and more activities with other kids, and that helped me a lot with my autism. It forced me to do some of the things I wasn't comfortable doing, and to do them over and over until I became comfortable doing them. But you can't grow out of autism. You can't cure it. There are no medicines you can take to make it go away, and now all my friends have graduated high school and gone off to college and I know I'm probably not ever going to college. I understand that. But the reason they're all going to college is to get a job, and I've already got a job. And it's a good job, too. I work at Wegmans, a local supermarket, and I hope to stay at that job, and to me that's a normal life. Maybe someday I'll get an apartment and live on my own, which is what all my friends will be doing, too.

But the big point I want to make in this chapter is that it's all about focus. That's really the most important thing. It doesn't matter if it's writing a book or giving a speech or meeting new people or playing a basketball game or sweeping up down at the store. Or baking bread. That's one of the things they have me doing now at work. They've got me in the bakery, baking fresh bread, and sometimes I take home a loaf of bread and I take a bite and think it's the best-tasting bread there ever was in the whole wide world. It tastes that way because I made it. It tastes that way because I learned how to do something new and now I can do it pretty good. So it doesn't matter what you're doing, just concentrate on doing a good job, you know. Just get it done. Do what people expect, and then do a little more, and after that do even more. Surprise them. Work hard. And stay focused. Always, always, always keep focused because, you know, you never know what might happen.

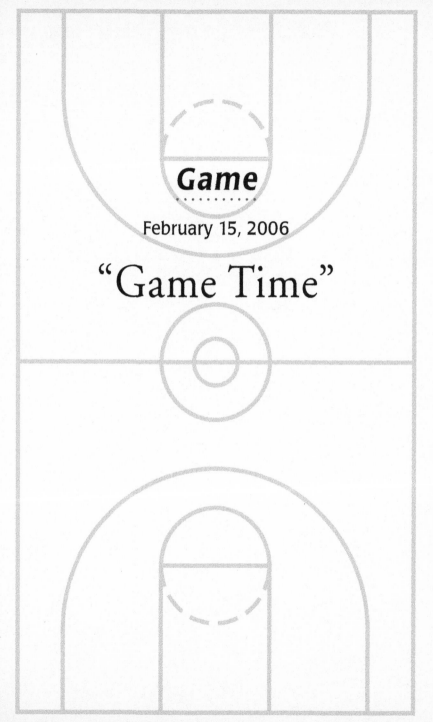

Game

February 15, 2006

"Game Time"

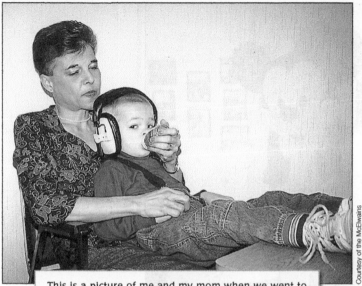

This is a picture of me and my mom when we went to
Connecticut for an experimental hearing treatment.

This is a picture of me and Josh
in our Halloween costumes.

We got to meet Mickey Mouse when
we went to Disney World.

Here I am at a cross-
country meet.

We're Number One! Me and the team.

Courtesy of Jay Shelofsky

This is a picture of me with
Coach Johnson.

Courtesy of Jay Shelofsky

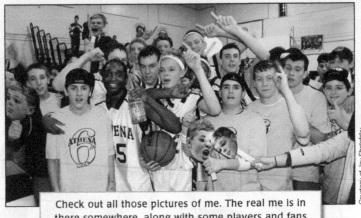

Check out all those pictures of me. The real me is in there somewhere, along with some players and fans after the Senior Night game.

I don't know if you've ever been carried off the court on your teammates' shoulders, but it's pretty cool.

The 6th Man section, cheering me on.

This is a bunch of different pictures of me as team manager. It was put together by our friend Jay Shelofsky, and it shows how crazy and emotional I used to get during our games.

J-Mac in Action
He is the man!!

Here we are celebrating our championship.

Me and the team, after our big win.

Here I am posing with all our cheerleaders at the Sectionals.

Me and my dad.

I'm smiling here because this was one of the first awards I ever got.

My parents are smiling too.

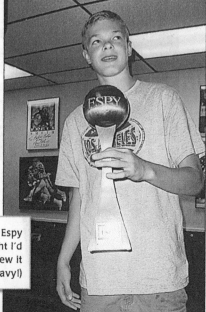

This is me holding my Espy Award. I never thought I'd win. (And I never knew it would be so heavy!)

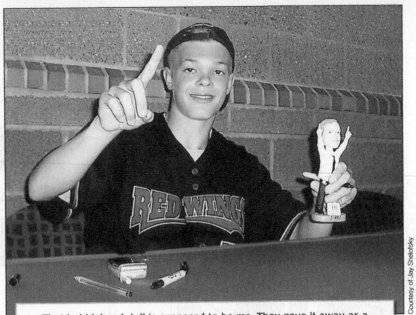

That bobblehead doll is supposed to be me. They gave it away as a souvenir at the Rochester Red Wings minor-league baseball game.

This is me at graduation. You can see I'm pretty excited.

I WASN'T NERVOUS ABOUT THE game getting started, but I was anxious. The difference was I knew if I got a chance to play I would probably hit a couple shots, but I wanted to find out what was going to happen. The Senior Night ceremony was great, but I wanted to get going already. I wanted to see how everything would turn out. So, yeah, I was anxious, but I don't really get nervous. Nervous is when you're not sure if you want something to happen, or if you're not sure how something will turn out, but here I was pretty sure. I was sure what I wanted, which was to get in the game, and I was sure what would happen if I did, which was I would find a way to get an open shot at the basket. I hoped like crazy it would go in, so this part I wasn't so sure about, but I knew I'd get my chance.

The gym was only half full when they started announcing all the seniors, but then during the shootaround people started to come in. Now the stands were almost full, and you could tell the people were also getting anxious. They wanted the game to start.

The kids up in the 6th Man section, they were stomping their feet on the bleachers, making a lot of noise. They were wearing these bright gold shirts they had made up, and that whole section where they were sitting, it really stood out. It was like a big bright golden sun shining down on the court.

One of the last things that had to happen before the game could start was the cheerleaders from each school had to do their opening cheers at center court. I always liked watching the cheerleaders, especially the ones from Greece Athena. I knew a lot of the girls, so sometimes they would smile or wave, but before this game I wasn't paying much attention to the cheerleaders. I was supposed to be paying attention to the game. The cheerleaders were just marching around, and jumping around, and clapping and cheering, and it was all a bunch of noise to me. I feel bad saying this, because a lot of the cheerleaders were my friends and I know they worked really hard on their cheers and it's supposed to get us pumped and everything, but I was too focused on the game to notice. Usually, I would clap and cheer along with them, but not on Senior Night. I'm sorry, but I had to concentrate on the game. I had to focus.

Then we lined up in front of our benches and stood for the national anthem. The whole gym was quiet, except for the person who was going to sing. Our cheerleaders were spread out in front of our basket and standing in a giant V formation, which I think was supposed to stand for "victory." This is what someone told me later. I can't think what else it could stand for. Maybe "valor." That's another word people use when they talk about sports. It's like courage.

I always liked this part of the game, because even though it was just a high school game it felt like a professional game, the way we were all standing for the national anthem. I liked the way our cheerleaders formed that giant V. It's like we were in the NBA, or at a big college game, instead of just in our high school gym. There was a lot of school spirit at Greece Athena. You could see it in the way the gym filled up for the game. You could see it in the way the kids in the 6th Man section wore their bright gold shirts and stomped their feet and cheered really loud. You could see it in the way the cheerleaders stood proudly in their giant V, for victory or valor or whatever.

And you could hear it in the way everyone cheered for our players when they announced our starting lineup. This was what happened next, but before they called out our team they said my name on the public-address system. They announced that I was a senior, and that this was my last game. I was out on the court, waiting to congratulate our starters, when they said my name on the loudspeaker. I didn't know they were going to do this, and it got a big cheer. I thought that was cool. People shouted out things like "Way to go, J-Mac!" That's one that stood out.

When everyone was announced, our team went to center court for the tip-off, and I sat down on the bench next to Coach Johnson. My dad said later I had the best seat in the house, and it's true. I did. But it wasn't really a seat for Coach Johnson. He didn't like to sit too much during our games. He liked to walk up and down the sidelines. I didn't want to be sitting, either. I was too anxious to be sitting. I wanted to jump up and down and cheer, like I usually did at our games, but when you're on the court like that, sitting with the team, sitting next to the coach, you can't jump up and cheer so much. Everyone used to tease me, when I was in my shirt and tie at one of our games, because after just a couple minutes of me jumping around so much my shirt was untucked and everything. My mom always liked me to look neat and presentable for games, but I was a mess once we got started.

My friend John Swartz took the jump ball for us, and the Spencerport center beat him on the jump but we controlled the tap anyway. That's always a good sign, when you get beat on the jump but still control the tap. That means you're hustling. That means the breaks will go your way. Steve Kerr got the ball in the far corner, wearing Matt Sheehan's jersey, and fired up a three, but he missed the rim entirely and Spencerport grabbed the rebound. Steve got the ball back at half court, though. We went into our half-court press, which was something Coach liked to do at the start of a game, to rattle the other team, and Steve stole the ball and got it in low to Rickey Wallace, who was one of our best players. He's the one whose big brother was John Wallace, the All-American at Syracuse who used to play in the NBA. Rickey drove across the lane and hit a layup to put us up 2–0. The ball bounced around the rim a little bit before going in, which is also a good sign. When that happens, it also means the breaks will go your way.

I thought, *Okay, this is our game to win*. I thought, *If we keep playing like this, Spencerport doesn't have a chance.*

It took us a while to find our rhythm, though. We kept stopping Spencerport on the defensive end, but we missed a couple shots and turned the ball over. A couple times, this happened. On our third or fourth time down the floor, John Swartz got the ball down low and put in a soft layup to put us up 4–0. He was fouled on the play, but he missed the free throw.

Spencerport called a time-out, because it seemed from these first couple minutes that we were going to run all over them, even though we were missing a lot of shots, and we got another stop when they came out of the time-out, and this time Steve Kerr found Rickey Wallace low and he hit another bucket to make it 6–0.

One of the guys on the bench leaned over to me and said, "At this rate, J, you'll be in before the first quarter is over." I don't remember who said this, but I didn't think this was true. I thought we were still a long way from taking control of the game. We were off to a good start, but it was early. Coach Johnson said we'd have to get out to a big lead before I'd see any time. He said all the other guys on the team would have to get in before I could get in, so I knew it wouldn't be for a while.

Then, on the next possession, the Spencerport guard took the ball in for an easy layup to make the score 6–2, but my friend Levar Goff answered with a three-pointer to make it 9–2. That's a big lead for so early in the game, but that's what we expected. I don't want to brag or anything, but we weren't too worried about Spencerport. We matched up against them pretty good. They were nice guys, a lot of them were friends of ours, but they didn't have a great season that year, and we'd won our first game against them in their gym about a month earlier.

I settled in on the bench next to Coach Johnson and our assistant coaches. I thought, *Okay, guys, all we have to do is settle down and play our game and hit our shots and we have a chance at the division.* I thought, *Okay, guys, stay focused.* I wasn't thinking about getting into the game. I mean, I was and I wasn't. It was in the back of my mind, but it wasn't in the front. It was something that might happen. Coach told me he'd do his best to find me a spot, but right now all I was thinking about was us taking control of the game and getting another win. It was a statement game for us. That's what you call a game like this. We'd already made it to the sectionals. We'd already been passed through to the second round. Now we had to finish our regular season with a big win and tell everyone in Monroe County basketball that we were the team to beat. That's why they call it a statement game, because you're telling everybody what you want them to know.

TWO
BIG BIRD

P EOPLE TELL ME I DIDN'T talk until I was five years
old, which I guess is a long time to wait to start talking. My mom and dad were getting pretty anxious,
wondering if I would ever get around to it. They were
worried about me. My mom said she used to cry sometimes,
thinking about what might be wrong with me, and then when
she knew what was wrong with me, she also cried. If you know
my mom you know it's not like her to cry, but she said she just
had to get it out. She went to her room and closed the door and
cried for a half hour. Then she was okay.

They didn't know at first what was wrong with me, but then
the doctors said I had autism. My parents didn't know a lot about
it, except they knew I wasn't talking. They knew I wouldn't let
them hold me, and that I kind of stiffened up if they tried to
touch me. I don't remember any of this, but I've heard the stories
enough times. I didn't like to be hugged or kissed, and I didn't
look at you when you talked to me. I never really laughed or

smiled. Everyone said it's like I was someplace else. In my head, I was someplace else. Sometimes I would wake up in the middle of the night and start running around the house, screaming. My eyes were open but I was still asleep, and my parents would have to hold me to keep me from screaming and running, but I didn't like to be held so this just made me scream even more. When I got older and bigger, it got harder for my mother to hold me and keep me still, but when I was little it was no problem. It was just a problem for my mother to catch me, because I was running around all over the place. She told me that once she dislocated her shoulder trying to hold me when I was running around and screaming. This was when I was older and bigger. I felt bad about this when she told me, even though she also told me it wasn't my fault. I couldn't help what I was doing and she was just trying to get me to calm down.

I was two and a half years old when they first used the word "autism" to describe what was wrong with me. My parents had never heard of autism before. My father said it sounded like something out of science fiction, and my mother did what she always did when she didn't know something. She read everything she could about it. My parents had been worried because I wasn't developing like my brother, Josh. The reason they were worried about this was because Josh was born three months too soon. The word for it is "premature." He wasn't finished growing—that's how it was always explained to me—and because he wasn't finished growing, he did things a little bit slower, a little bit later than other kids his age. Walking, talking, eating . . . whatever babies do, he took a little longer to do it, and then I came and took even longer. Actually, I walked earlier than Josh. I walked at about a year. Josh walked at about fourteen months. So that's two months earlier that I walked. This is according to what my mother always told us. But the other stuff, I did way later than my brother. Talking, toilet training, reading and writing, playing with other kids . . . it took me a lot longer. All they had to compare me to was Josh, so at first they didn't think there was anything wrong with me because he was slow doing these things, too. They just thought this was the regular way kids grew and learned. But then I went past how old Josh was when he started doing these things, and then after a while they'd see other kids talking and playing, and they'd wonder why I wasn't like that, talking and playing.

Our pediatrician said to give it some time. His name was Dr. Vora. He was my doctor for the whole time when I was little. He's still my doctor. He said this during my regular checkups, because at first we only went in for my regular checkups. He said some children develop in different ways. He said there was no reason to worry just yet and that he would keep checking on me. I don't remember feeling like anyone was worried about me, or knowing that my mother was in her room crying, or even feeling frustrated that I couldn't make myself understood. I was just a baby. Maybe I didn't have anything to say—that's the way I look at it now, because talking, it's not that big a deal. When I had something to say, I talked.

One of the things Dr. Vora suggested was that I wasn't talking because Josh was doing all the talking. Josh talked a lot. My mother says he was a regular Gabby Hayes. I don't know who this is, but it's probably someone who talked a lot. That was Josh. Dr. Vora said it was possible that I wasn't talking because Josh was doing all the talking for me. We were always together, and Dr. Vora said it would be a good idea to put me in day care, away from Josh, and to see if I started to talk. The idea was maybe I would be forced to do some of these things on my own if Josh wasn't around. This was when I was about a year and a half, before they had me tested, before anyone even mentioned autism. Everybody was still thinking I was normal, just slow to talk, and this seemed like a good idea, so my mother signed me up for a day-care program next to Wegmans, the supermarket where I now work. This was just a regular day-care place, for regular kids. How she found it was it was on her way to the supermarket. She set it up so she could drop me off, and then go into the supermarket with Josh to do her shopping. I went once a week, on Thursdays, and stayed for a couple hours while they shopped, and the whole time I just sat in the corner by myself. This was what they told my mother. This went on for maybe a year, and all I did was sit by myself in the corner, the whole time.

DAVID McELWAIN (father)

When he was real little, Jason had night screams. Night terrors, some people call them. He never slept through the night. We were exhausted all the time from staying up with him and chasing him around the house. Our big thing was that he didn't wake up Josh. It was bad enough we had one of them up all night. We didn't want the other one up all night, too.

Jason also had this chewing problem. You know how you feed kids baby food when they're first born? Well, that's all Jason would eat, and he never learned how to chew. We talked to the pediatrician about it. He just wasn't eating. We'd give him food of substance and he'd just spit it out. Then we had to cut everything into tiny pieces, but he'd spit this out, too. He'd start crying, and having one of his outbursts.

This would be a problem for Jason until he was older, maybe six or seven. My wife was like a drill sergeant, trying to get him to eat. She'd say, "Eat, eat, eat." She was always on him about it. She'd sit right there with him, until he finished. Or she'd have to force-feed him. It was always a struggle, always a battle. My wife was always the type, you put a plate of food in front of the kids, she expected them to eat. We ate together every night, as soon as I got home from work, but my wife didn't spend too much time eating. She was always feeding Jason, always pestering him to eat. I'll tell you, meals were not fun in our house. They could be difficult.

Finally, when I was about two and a half, my parents had me tested. They knew something was wrong and it wasn't just that I was developing slowly. They knew I wasn't just being difficult. This was when they said I had autism. The running around and screaming in the middle of the night was called an autistic outburst. I had different kinds of these, not just in the middle of the night. Sometimes I would flap my arms up and down and all around, like a bird. Sometimes I would just kick and scream. Sometimes I would just run around, out of control. But the not talking, that was the biggest thing, the most serious thing. The doctors told my parents that if I didn't talk by a certain age it would tell them how serious my autism was going to be. Everything had to do with when I started talking. Some doctors told my parents I might never talk. This was one of the times my mother went into her room and cried. She told me about this when I was older. I feel bad about this now, that my mother was crying because of me, but she wasn't so used to the idea back then, the idea of me being autistic. She got used to it, I think, once she saw I could be like a regular kid, too. I could be normal about some things and autistic about some things and I don't think she cried so much after a while.

My dad wasn't too worried about this. That was his personality. He looked at everything in a positive way. He calls himself a glass-half-full kind of person. He calls my mom a glass-half-empty kind of person, because she looks at everything in a negative way. She said my dad was refusing to accept how I was, but he just thought I would talk when I had something to say. That's a good way to look at it, don't you think? My mom, she was superworried. She was on a mission to get me to talk. Everything she did was to get me to talk, because the doctors said this would decide about everything that happened next. The story she tells now is that I used to point a lot to make myself understood. I tugged on her clothes to get her attention. If I wanted a bottle, I pointed to a bottle. If I wanted something to eat, I pointed to it. And each time she would make me say the word for what I wanted. She would make me say it in baby talk, because that's how she would say it. She would say, "Ba-ba," for when I wanted a bottle. She would say, "Wa-wa," for when I wanted water. I was already two and three and four years old, but the words she used were the words she used with Josh, when he was starting to talk. That's the way she knew to teach someone to talk. Over and over, she'd say these words in baby talk, trying to get me to say them the same way. She said sometimes she used to work on me for fifteen minutes, trying to get me to say something, and then she'd finally give up and give me the bottle, or whatever it was. If I tugged on her clothes to get her attention, she said, "Ma." Over and over, she said this, too. "Ma." She pointed to herself when she said this, so I would make the connection. She did the same thing for my dad. She pointed to him and said, "Da." Over and over. My father was supposed to do this, too, whenever I was with him, but he wasn't so patient about it as my mother. He would do it at first, but he wouldn't make me wait fifteen minutes. He would just give me whatever I was pointing to, without making me wait or say the right word. Of course, I don't remember this, but this was what everyone in my family always said.

It's hard for me to tell what it's like to be autistic, because it's just who I am. Also, I don't really remember how I was when I was little, just like most people don't remember how they were when they were little, so here I'm going to let one of the people who tested me when I was four years old tell how I was. I don't remember this person, but this was what she wrote in one of the reports my father saved in my medical file.

MARIANNE MOODY (speech-language pathologist, Board of Cooperative Educational Services)

Jason engages in repetitive play most of the time. For example, he will open and close the door on the playhouse, click together play food, and tap markers on the table. He enjoys tactile materials, such as the sand and birdseed table, cornmeal trays, and the macaroni table. He does not like to touch Play-Doh, but rather tends to use the cookie cutters and wooden rolling pins to tap or click together. He also likes to draw with the markers on paper, but at times he stops drawing and starts to tap the markers, rather than use them appropriately.

Jason does not feed himself. He eats pureed foods and some table foods, such as French toast, pancakes, green beans, peas, and ice cream sandwiches. These are all fed to him on a spoon by his mother. He drinks from a bottle and a lidded cup at home. He uses a lidded cup at school. Jason does not yet finger-feed, but will touch Cheerios, crackers, and cookies. He tends to crumble them in his hands if given whole. Jason sits with the class at snack time and is very aware of the food that is offered for snack. He will often watch and maintain eye contact with an adult who is eating and will open and close his mouth while doing so.

Like I said, I don't remember any of this, but it's what this person wrote. I also don't remember too much stuff that happened at home when I was little, except for the stories I've been told, like how reading to me was one of my mother's big things. She read to Josh, too, but she read to me all the time. Like an hour or so a day. Sometimes with Josh and sometimes just by myself. Big picture books, with simple words that matched the big pictures. Storybooks with simple stories that repeated the same words and phrases, over and over. Also, I didn't have a lot of toys as a little kid, but the few toys I had were all talking toys. Josh's toys were also talking toys, because my mother thought I would play with them, too. Remember those See 'n Say toys, where you turned a pointer to a farm animal and then pulled a string and it said the name of the farm animal and the sound it made? They had them for other things, too, like jungle animals or different kinds of trucks. Those were the kinds of toys she'd buy for us, hoping to get me to talk. The toys with strings you could pull to get them to talk. Everything had to have a lesson in it, a way to help me with my autism.

Whatever she tried, I wouldn't respond. The only things my parents tried that I reacted to were swimming and lights. They found out about these by accident, and that's what I'll tell about now. My mom and dad were big swimmers when I was little. They used to take us to the pool every weekend, and they said I loved the water. My grandparents lived at a place where there was a pool, and that's where we would go. Josh didn't like to swim, but I just splashed around the whole time. If they weren't watching me, or if I didn't have my floaties on or this bubble I used to have to wear, I would just jump in anyway. A couple times my dad had to jump in after me because I didn't really know how to swim. Everyone said I wasn't afraid of the water, and I guess I wasn't because I just kept jumping in. This was because when you have autism you're not afraid of anything. The part of your brain that gets afraid, it doesn't really work so good. So my parents just had to be extracareful when I was swimming, but even though they had to be extracareful this was still very exciting for my parents, that I was swimming and that I wasn't afraid of the water, because it was the first time I responded to anything. Dr. Vora said it was a positive thing.

The other thing I responded to was lights. It turned out that when they flicked the lights on and off in the house, it would get me to drink or eat or whatever. I didn't eat at all when I was little. Everything they gave me, they had to force-feed me, but then one day the light went on and off, and I started to suck from my bottle, so they did it again. It was an accident that they figured this out, but it was an accident that turned into a plan. I was with my grandmother when this happened the first time. I don't know how she figured out the connection, but she told my mother and the two of them ran around the house, turning the lights on and off, and from then on whenever I had to eat, they sat near a switch or a lamp or something and turned the lights on and off. This went on for a long time, that they had to feed me this way.

The longer I didn't talk, the more everyone worried I would never talk. And then one day, I talked. The story my parents tell is that I was sitting in the living room with Josh, watching *Sesame Street*. He really loved *Sesame Street*. I didn't care about *Sesame Street* too much. I just wanted to be with Josh. It probably didn't even matter to me what we were watching, just that we were watching. Probably I wasn't even looking at the screen. I was holding a little blanket I used to carry with me all the time. My parents called it my "Mimi." I don't know where they got that from, but that's what they called it, and for a long time when I was little, I was never without my Mimi. It was really a cloth diaper, but everyone said it was a blanket. They also told me I used to carry around two unopened packs of Trident gum, which I would clap together all the time. That was my main toy. A lot of times, with autism, you can get really stuck on something, and I don't know how it happened but I was stuck on these packs of gum. It was in pink packages, the bubble gum kind. I'd just clap them together, all day long. If one of the packs broke, my parents would get me another. They used to keep all these packs around the house, because they kept breaking, from all the banging together. I don't know what they did with all the gum. That would be interesting to find out, what happened to all that gum.

DEBBIE McELWAIN (mother)

We didn't believe in a lot of television in our house. We didn't even have cable when the boys were little, but on Sunday mornings the local PBS station would run three hours of *Sesame Street*, and my husband would tape it for them and they'd watch that tape during the week.

Four o'clock or so on a Thursday afternoon, I was in the kitchen making dinner, and Josh comes running in saying, "Mommy, Jason spoke." What he said was, "Big Bird." That's all. He just pointed to the television when Big Bird came on and said, "Big Bird."

This was very important because the doctors kept telling us that if you could get an autistic child to speak, even if it's just one word, you can maybe get him to open up and start to communicate. That's what we'd been working on. It was our first real goal for Jason, so when Josh came into the kitchen I dropped whatever I was doing and ran back out into the living room to see for myself. I was so excited. And there was Jason, on the floor in front of the couch, banging his two packs of Trident together, staring at the television.

I kneeled down in front of him and put his face in my hands. That's what they taught us, to get Jason to pay attention. You just cup his face in your hands and get in real close and try to get him to look right at you, and I kept saying, "Big Bird, Big Bird, Big Bird." I was like a crazy woman. And he just kept staring back at me with this blank look, but I kept at it. "Big Bird, Big Bird, Big Bird."

Finally, just over my shoulder, Big Bird came back on the television, and I guess Jason could see it even though I was in real close, and he opened his mouth and said it again: "Big Bird." Just like a regular kid. And I think I screamed, or cried, or jumped up and down—that's how big a moment it was for our family.

I got right on the phone and called my husband, because he of course knew what it meant, and after that, I think I called my mother. I called everyone I knew. It was the most exciting thing. I don't even remember what happened to dinner that night, when I got back to the kitchen, because Jason talking was a real breakthrough for us. For that one night anyway, dinner wasn't so important.

My mother still does that thing where she puts my face in her hands. She did it that night on the basketball court, after I scored all those points and the place was going crazy. I don't know where she learned this from. Maybe she read about it in an article. Or maybe it's just something she figured out by herself. She says it helps me to concentrate, but really it just makes me mad. I hope it doesn't hurt her feelings when she reads this, but it does, I'm sorry. She thinks I'm paying better attention to her when she's in my face like that, but really I'm just waiting for her to let me go. I don't like it. And besides, I can hear her just fine from across the room, like she talks to everyone else. She's pretty loud, my mother. Of course I can hear her. All you have to do is meet her one time and listen to her talk and you'll know I can hear her.

Anyway, that's the story of me talking for the first time, and from there I just kept it going. I said, "Ma" and "Da" and "Josh," just like a toddler, and from there it was only a little bit of time until I was speaking in full sentences and really talking. Now sometimes, for a joke, my mother will say she liked it better when I didn't talk so much, but I know she doesn't mean it. I know she just means I shouldn't talk so much, and then I want to make a joke of it myself, and remind her that she was the one who made such a big deal out of it, jumping up and down like that, calling everybody on the phone. I ask her to tell me the story about me saying "Big Bird" for the first time, and her going crazy like she did, and I think, *Well, what did you expect?*

Even before I started talking, they put me in special-education training. In my house, we called it special ed. It was something they had in Rochester for people with autism and other disabilities. It was run by Monroe County, and I was allowed to go when I was three years old. It was a BOCES program. BOCES is the initials for Board of Cooperative Educational Services. They have BOCES programs all over New York State. They do special things for students with special needs, extra things that their regular schools can't do. As soon as I was allowed to go, my parents started sending me. The kids there were all different. Some of them had learning disabilities. Some of them had physical disabilities. Some of them had autism, or cerebral palsy. There was one kid who was deaf, so he was learning sign language, and the rest of us would watch and learn sign language, too. I wasn't talking yet, but I could understand some of the signs. I still remember how to sign, but I don't do it too much so I've forgotten a lot of it.

Every year, I went to a different school, depending on where they had the program that was best for what I had. One year, I had to travel almost an hour on the bus to a place called Churchville. It wasn't really an hour away, but the bus had to make a lot of stops. It picked me up at my house at seven o'clock in the morning, and it dropped me off really late, like four thirty or five o'clock in the afternoon. Other times, there was a school closer to my house that had the right program for me, so that's where I went. I never really made any friends at these schools. I mean, I was friendly with the other kids, but we didn't see each other outside of school. I wasn't really social, which is funny, because later on, when I was older, I was very social. I was always talking and saying hello and meeting new people, but when I was little all the kids in my classes were so different from each other. Some of them talked, and some of them didn't. Some of them played, and some of them didn't. My parents would come to class for a special event or activity and my father would leave feeling a little bit better about my autism, because it seemed to him I was better off than a lot of the other kids. He compared how I was to how they were. He said I was higher-functioning. My mother would leave feeling a little worse that I was stuck in a classroom all day with kids who weren't as high-functioning as me. This is a good example of the glass-half-empty and the glass-half-full ideas my parents had, of how they could see the same things in different ways. I was somewhere in the middle, and to my mom this was a bad thing and to my dad this was a good thing.

One of the things that was like a highlight in my family was we went to Disney World. I think I was two and a half. We went later, when I was eight, and then when I was thirteen, but I don't really remember that first time, other than the pictures. My brother, Josh, doesn't really remember it either. We were both really little. That first time we went, it was January and I had to wear a winter coat when we went to the airport in Rochester, and then it was warm when we got to Disney World, so I had to take my coat off. This was probably confusing to me, but it was probably confusing to Josh, too, and he was normal. There are pictures of us in the Magic Kingdom, and pictures of us with Captain Hook. Josh really wanted to see Captain Hook. We had the *Peter Pan* video at home, and he liked to watch it all the time. We were just like a regular family, even though I had autism, and there was one time, when we were a whole bunch older, and we were looking at some of the pictures, Josh asked my parents why they took us if they knew we wouldn't remember it. They said it was because they wanted us to be like a regular family, even though we weren't. This was what regular families did—they went to Disney World.

When I got older, I used to look at the pictures from Disney World and wish I could remember them, because I always wanted to go to Disney World. It's like I didn't really go, because I couldn't remember, but then we finally did go again, only it wasn't so easy to take me to a place like Disney World once I got older. This was what my parents always said. By the time I was three years old, they said it was hard for them to take me away from home like that, to a new place, with so many people. They couldn't predict how I would react. But they took me anyway, those two more times, and I don't think I gave them too much trouble. Maybe I had some autistic outbursts or something, and maybe I wasn't as "normal" as I was when I was only two and a half, and those trips I remember. When I got older, whatever amusement park I went to, Disney World or the amusement parks near my house, I went on all the rides. All the biggest roller coasters. That first time at Disney World, I don't think I went on any rides because I was too little, but after that I went on everything. Whatever I was tall enough to ride, that's what I went on.

Another thing I remember is that I went for a lot of tests. I went to a place called Strong Memorial. It's a hospital where they test you for all different things. They had five different doctors examine me. It took two whole days. My mother stayed with me the whole time. There was someone to check my hearing, someone to check my speech. A different doctor for every way my body and my brain were supposed to work. And what they found after all these tests was that my autism was severe. They said also my kind of autism was very rare. Only one person in every ten thousand people gets it, so it's not a lot. This really upset my mother. She didn't want me to have something so rare, or so severe. She told me later that this was one of the times she went in her room and cried, after we got back from Strong Memorial that second day.

Also, my parents said that one of the things that really bothered me when I was little was my hearing. My ears were very sensitive. This happens a lot with autistic kids. If there was a garbage truck out in the street, I'd scream and cover my ears. If my mother ran the blender or the vacuum cleaner too close to me, I'd scream and cover my ears. It was very painful for me to hear these loud, banging noises. Anything sudden, any kind of noise that would make a normal person jump, I really hated. The doctors said that my ears were sensitive, and that loud, sudden noises caused me a lot of pain. I don't remember feeling the pain, but this is what my parents learned about it. My mother's idea for how to get me out of this problem was to just keep running the blender and the vacuum cleaner. She thought I would just get used to it and then it wouldn't be a problem anymore, but it was still a problem. In fact, it got worse as I got older. My hearing got more and more sensitive.

DEBBIE McELWAIN

I got a lot of my ideas from reading, from television. All along, I just refused to accept Jason's diagnosis. I accepted it, but I also got past it. Whatever the textbooks said, whatever the experts said, I thought Jason would be different. All I knew was that I would try anything to get him normal. Sometimes, I would do the opposite of what the doctors said because it made more sense. For example, before he was speaking there was this new thing called Facilitative Speaking. The idea was you taught the child to talk through a computer. And I wouldn't let them do it with Jason. I said no. I didn't want him to have a crutch. I knew if he learned to speak by using this device, he'd never learn to speak on his own. This was my own personal belief. It went against the experts, but I didn't care. This was my kid.

They also wanted him on Ritalin. He didn't have a good attention span and they thought this would help. I said no. I said once he started speaking maybe I would allow it, on the lowest dose possible, to help him learn, to help his concentration, but to me this was just another crutch. I don't believe in crutches. I wouldn't let my son Josh use a calculator at home or at school, and now he's studying math in college, so you tell me.

And then there was the problem with his hearing. It was a real problem. I thought I could just force him out of it, get him used to loud noises so they wouldn't bother him anymore. And it was while this was going on that I saw a report on *20/20*. It was about a desensitization treatment for hearing that was supposed to help kids like Jason. It was called Auditory Hearing Training, I think. It was developed by a doctor in San Diego. They put headphones on the patient and played some sort of music and changed the volume over a period of time to tone down the hearing process.

This was on a Friday night, that I saw the report on television. By Saturday morning, I knew where the closest facility was, where they were doing this treatment, what it would cost, everything. It was at a place in New Hartford, Connecticut, so I immediately made an appointment. They couldn't take us for two months, but I made the appointment right away, and when it came time for the appointment, we all went to Connecticut to have Jason tested. So I would try anything. I wouldn't do everything the doctors said, but I would listen to everything and decide what was best for Jason.

My parents still talk about that trip to Connecticut. It was like a family highlight, but a highlight makes it sound like a good thing. I don't think it was such a good thing, but it stands out. Everyone remembers it. I don't remember it, but Josh does. He was old enough. He remembers it like an adventure. So it's that kind of highlight, an adventure kind of highlight. We had to go for two weeks, all four of us. My mother wasn't going to leave Josh and my father home in Greece. She wasn't going to leave Josh with my grandparents. Usually, my grandparents helped take care of us, like if my mother had to work or something, but not for that long. My mother liked to have everyone together. She just announced one day we were all going to Connecticut. My father said he had no idea what hit him. It was a big thing, for my parents to take off from work, for my dad especially. He had a good job, but he didn't have a lot of vacation time. This was his vacation time. I don't know about you, but I wouldn't want to spend my vacation time at a clinic in Connecticut for two weeks. No way. Also, we had to stay in a motel for the whole time, in one room. We stayed at a Super 8. Other than those times we went to Disney World, it was the only time we stayed in a motel or a hotel, until one other time when I was older when we went to Washington, D.C.

The way it worked was I would go into the clinic with my mother for a half hour each morning and a half hour each afternoon. For fourteen days, we did this. It wasn't a test or anything. It was a treatment. It was supposed to make my hearing better, and less sensitive. I worked with the same doctor every day. My father would stay behind with Josh in the motel, or they would wait for us in the waiting room. I was supposed to sit on my mom's lap while the doctor put these big headphones on me. I didn't like these headphones. They made me feel like they were swallowing up my head, like I was wearing a helmet. I still don't like headphones too much. All my friends, they listen to their iPods or whatever, but I don't like it when you put the music right into your ear. It's annoying. But back when I was little, I really, really didn't like it. I kept ripping the headphones off my head. My mom said I used to fight her when she tried to put them on, and for the first visit or two, I kept ripping them off, and they kept putting them back on, but after a while I got used to them. After a while it got so I could keep them on for the whole thirty-minute treatment. It was thirty minutes in the morning, and then another thirty minutes in the afternoon. They played music. They turned the volume up and down. They changed all the sounds.

I don't really know if the treatment worked, because I think I still had trouble with my hearing. My ears were still sensitive. It still hurt to hear a sharp, loud, banging sound. But it's important to mention this trip because it shows all the different things my parents would try to help me get better. It shows how we would all go to a motel for two weeks to try a new treatment because my mother heard about it on television, even though my dad had to miss two weeks of work and everything.

DAVID McELWAIN

My wife wasn't sold on this hearing treatment, but it was still in the experimental stage and it was becoming more and more popular. In a lot of the magazines she was reading, people were talking about it, so when they opened up a clinic for it in Rochester, she signed Jason up again. I ended up taking Jason to this round of treatments, because by this time Debbie was working part-time and she wanted to be home to get Josh off the bus each day after school.

That's how we did a lot of Jason's treatment. We were unconventional. We didn't have a mental health professional guiding us. We just had our regular pediatrician and we kind of stumbled through and put together our own treatment. My wife would read something, and we would give it a try. If it didn't work the first time, maybe we would try it again. Or maybe we wouldn't. We don't have any secrets to share about how to care for an autistic child. Whatever made sense, we just gave it a try. That's all.

This second time we tried the hearing treatment, Jason was five years old. We paid another $1,000, which was what it cost. Our insurance wouldn't cover it, but we paid it anyway. My in-laws helped us out. I took Jason twice each day for another fourteen days, another thirty minutes in the morning and thirty minutes in the afternoon, and even then it wasn't like a light switch went off or anything. Even then it wasn't like all of a sudden he wasn't sensitive to certain sounds. It was more of a gradual thing.

The thing about the trip to Connecticut, though, was all the time I spent in the waiting room with Josh, looking at all the other kids. This was the first time I really noticed that Jason wasn't the only one cupping his ears like that, he wasn't the only one rocking back and forth. He wasn't the only one having outbursts. Of course, I knew all these things. I read all the articles and saw that Jason's type of autism affected a lot of kids, a lot of families, but here in this waiting room was where I really noticed it. This was where it really hit home.

I wish I could tell more about when I was little, but all I remember is what I've been told since I got older. I remember the highlights, like I've written about. The highlights can be good things or bad things, it doesn't matter. They're just the things that stand out, the stories we talk about in our family, over and over. I remember that I didn't talk until I was about five. I remember that I didn't communicate, other than to point, and this was only when I really, really wanted something. I remember that when I first went to school I basically just sat there in the corner. I didn't do much of anything. I didn't play with the other special-ed kids, and I didn't respond to the kinds of things that other little kids respond to, other than the sudden, loud noises, which I really responded to, only not in a good way. I remember also that I wasn't toilet trained until I was six or seven. This is embarrassing, but I think I should mention it because there are a lot of autistic kids who have a problem with this. There's nothing to be embarrassed about. The doctors kept telling my parents not to worry too much because autistic kids eventually train themselves to go to the bathroom. It's just that it took me a long time to do it. For a while, when I was about six, I was good enough to go to the bathroom by myself during the day, but I still had to wear a night diaper, and then one time, when we were on a trip to Washington, D.C., my parents forgot to put a night diaper on me. This was one of the few other times we went on a trip and stayed overnight in a hotel or motel. My father thought my mother had put the night diaper on. My mother thought my father had put the night diaper on. And we woke up in the morning and there was no night diaper on, but it didn't matter because I was dry. So that was the end of my night diapers.

This was around when things really started to change for me and my family. I started to talk. I stopped wearing diapers. I started becoming more and more social. I started learning more at school, because once I started to talk they thought I could start to learn. This was when my mother allowed them to start me on a medicine called Ritalin, which was supposed to help me learn. The whole time, she was saying they could put me on it once I started to talk, but she didn't like us to take medicine. Even for things like headaches and colds, she didn't like us to take medicine. So she told them to put me on the lowest dose, and even this she started cutting in half without telling Dr. Vora or my teachers about it. She even cut it out entirely, and then about six months later she went in for a teacher conference and the teacher said how much better I was doing in school now that I was taking this medicine. My mother doesn't usually laugh a lot, but she said she laughed about this because she had taken me off the medicine six months earlier.

The special-ed teachers, they really cared about the kids in their class. They were really excited when one of us showed progress in some area. They made it so we were all excited for each other. They made it like a celebration, if one of us could suddenly recognize a letter or do a new kind of math problem. They tried to make it fun. A lot of my friends in these special-ed classes, we'd cheer each other on and help each other out just like regular kids in regular classes. The only difference was that we were autistic or learning disabled or we had some other thing wrong that made it so we couldn't think or concentrate like the regular kids.

The biggest change that came around this time was Josh started paying attention to me. Until I started talking, we didn't really hang out or anything. My mother would put us in the same room when we were little, watching television. Or she would read to us together. But he didn't bother with me much until now. Now we could be like brothers, and we could fight like brothers, and hang out together like brothers. Now I could do some of the things he always did, like play baseball and walk around the neighborhood.

This is the part I'll write about next.

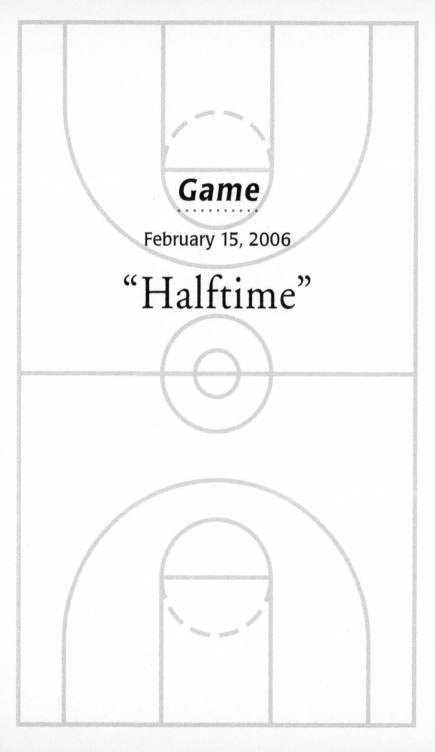

Game

February 15, 2006

"Halftime"

ALL IT TAKES IN A game like this is for someone to get hot. The Spencerport Rangers, they were playing us tight and tough, but they kept missing some easy layups and some short-range jumpers. They were getting their stops, and keeping us close, but they couldn't get into any kind of rhythm and neither could we. It was one of those games. We were up and down the court a couple times without scoring, but then we were down and back without giving up a basket, so the game kind of stood still. That's what it felt like, like we were standing still. We were winning, but not by much. We were in control, but not by much.

Then, about midway through the first quarter, my friend Steve Kerr began to heat up. That's how they talk about it in basketball. They say you're heating up. It means you're hot, like you can't miss, and when Steve gets going, he can really get going. He hit a three-pointer to put us up 12–4, and then after a stop he hit another jumper to make it 14–4. Then the teams traded baskets so we ended the first quarter up 16–8, which seems almost like a dominating score, but it didn't feel that way at the time. Usually when you score twice as many points as the other team it means you're playing twice as good as them, but it didn't matter what it said on the scoreboard. It still didn't feel like we were putting Spencerport away the way we needed to, to make a statement going into the sectionals. We were winning, but we weren't dominating.

Coach Johnson wasn't too happy during our team huddle after the first quarter. He wasn't upset, but he wasn't happy. He liked it when we dominated games, when we came into a time-out or a break between quarters with some kind of momentum. But here we had no momentum. We were just scratching out a lead. On the loudspeaker, they were playing "Who Are You?" by the Who, and one of my friends told me later it was a weird song for them to be playing, because at the same time Coach was telling us to step it up and start playing like we were out to win the sectional title. I didn't think of this connection myself, but Coach was challenging us to start playing like he knew we could play, like we wanted the game to say something about the kind of team we were, and then at the same time the Who was singing "Who Are You?" They play that song a lot for us at our home games. It's one of our main songs, so really it was just a coincidence that it came on at this time in the game, but the song really fit the first quarter. Things happen that way sometimes, the pieces just fit like it was all planned out before.

Steve Kerr sat down next to me on the bench to start the second quarter, and we talked a little bit about the game. We talked about starting to hit our shots and getting our stops and trying to pull away. We talked about how we had to take control.

Nothing against Spencerport. They had some pretty good play-ers. They were a great group of guys. But we wanted to come out strong and put the game away. Unfortunately, the Rangers scored first, to bring the score to 16–10, but then Levar Goff followed with another three-pointer to make it 19–10.

I liked having Steve Kerr next to me on the bench. He was one of my best friends on the team. Him and Brian Benson and Rickey Wallace and Levar Goff. Brian I knew my whole life. He lived on my street. We grew up playing sports together. Baseball, golf, swimming, basketball . . . whatever they had for us kids to play, we'd sign up and play. We rode our bikes together all the time, once my mother let me start riding around the neighbor-hood without some grown-up watching me. Steve and Rickey and Levar I didn't meet until high school, but we hung out a lot, except during games we didn't usually get a chance to hang out because they were always on the floor. That's what it felt like on the bench to start the second quarter, like me and Steve were hanging out, watching a game on television, only when we were talking about what our team needed to do it wasn't just the team we were rooting for, it was our team. It was the team we were playing for. And we weren't watching it on television. It was right there in front of us.

After Levar hit his three, we were called for a blocking foul when one of the Spencerport players tried to drive the lane, and Coach Johnson stood up and started to pace. This was what he did when he was frustrated. I know because I watched him dur-ing all our games, for two seasons. Like I wrote earlier, he didn't sit down a lot during our games. Whenever he stood up, it was usually because he didn't like how we were playing. He wasn't one of those coaches who yelled a lot from the bench, but when he stood up you knew he had something to say. If he stood up, it meant there was something about our game he wanted to fix. And then once he was up, he usually stayed up. It's like he'd forget to sit back down.

The Spencerport player only hit one of his free throws, to bring it to 19–11, and then the next time down the court we were fouled and hit both free throws to go back up 21–11. At some point in there, Coach Johnson sat back down—I guess because we had started to play a little bit better. Whatever he had seen and didn't like had somehow fixed itself. At least, we weren't making any mistakes.

Then Steve Kerr and Brian Benson went into the game. Brian was only a tenth-grader, and he didn't play a whole lot that season. Toward the end of the year, he started getting some minutes, but in the beginning he didn't play so much. He's really good, though. The next year, he'd be one of the best players on the team, so I was always happy for him when he got into the game. I liked it when we played well as a team, but I also liked it when my friends did well. I was rooting for both things to happen. And I knew once I got out there, they'd be rooting for me, too. That's how it is with teammates. You pick each other up. You cheer each other on. You work together to try to get the win.

Rickey Wallace hit a wide-open jumper to make it 23–11, and for the first time, it started to feel like we had some momentum. To everyone in the gym, that's how it felt. You know how it gets sometimes at a game when things start to turn in favor of one team. High school, college, pro . . . it doesn't matter. Everything just starts to go one team's way, and that's what started to happen. We opened up a pretty big lead. The Spencerport coach called a time-out, which I thought was a good time-out, because he didn't want the game to get away from his team. If I was the coach, I would have called a time-out here, too. During this time-out, they played "We Will Rock You" by Queen on the loudspeaker. It's one of those big stadium sports songs that they always play at basketball games and football games, so it felt like we were in a professional game. It's also one of our main songs, and the people in the gym were really into it. Everyone was clapping and stomping their feet on the bleachers. I don't know if you've ever heard it, but when a bunch of people stomp their feet on the bleachers they have in high school gyms, it makes a lot of noise. And these were the new metal bleachers, not the old wooden kind, so it sounded like thunder, a little bit.

Spencerport came out of the time-out, and one of their players drove the lane for a layup to make it 23–13, but then Rickey Wallace hit a three-pointer to make it 26–13. Our guys actually moved the ball pretty good on that possession, until they found Rickey for an open look, and Rickey just drained it. We had a couple guys like that on the team, guys like Rickey and Levar and Steve, guys who if you give them an open look they'd usually make the shot. Those were my favorite kinds of players, because they could burn the other team. That's the kind of player I wanted to be, the kind where if you gave me a little too much room I could burn you.

After this basket, coming just after that "We Will Rock You" time-out, the crowd was getting loud. A lot of the 6th Man kids kept stomping on the bleachers, trying to help with our momentum. Sometimes you hear them say on the news that the crowd was really into the game, and that's how it seemed. At 26–13, we'd doubled up on the score, and people were starting to get excited. It felt for the first time like we had control of the game, and it was at this time that the kids in the 6th Man section started chanting my name. Anyway, this was the first time I heard it. At first they started in with the same cheer they did for me back when I was on junior varsity, hitting those three free throws: "J-Mac!" *Clap, clap.* "J-Mac!" *Clap, clap.* And then they switched it up, so that they drew out my name really long, without the clapping. "Jayyyyy-Mac! Jayyyyy-Mac!" Over and over. It almost sounded like a kind of teasing.

"Jayyyyy-Mac!"

But it didn't sound like teasing to me. It sounded like cheering. It sounded like they were calling to me from across a big space, or maybe like they were calling me into the game. Other than that one time in that junior varsity game a couple years earlier, it was the only time a group of kids was cheering for me, calling for me. It made me feel good, that these kids wanted to see me play, and now that we'd doubled up the score they thought it was a good time for Coach to get me into the game. But Coach wasn't ready to put me in just yet. He didn't tell me anything about it, but I knew he'd have to get all his regular players into the game before he got me into the game, and there were still a bunch of players on the bench who hadn't gotten in yet. That was fair. That was the right thing to do. If I was the coach, that's how I would have done it. These guys had been on the team all year long. Some of them didn't get a lot of minutes. Some of them were seniors. As much as I wanted to play, it wouldn't be right for me to play ahead of them. I understood that. Like I said, I'm not dumb. I know how it works in sports. I know what's fair. Plus, these other guys were more experienced than me, and we were only up by thirteen points, and there was still a lot of time left in the game.

But even though I understood all these things, it still sounded pretty good to hear all these kids calling out my name. "Jayyyyy-Mac! Jayyyyy-Mac!" I thought about my parents, sitting up in the stands, my mom holding the flowers I'd given her during the Senior Night ceremony, listening to all these kids call my name. I thought it would make them proud. I wondered if they were calling out my name, too.

We traded baskets again, and with the score at 28–15 in our favor, the first half was winding down. Rickey Wallace had just hit a jumper, and the Spencerport guard was racing up the court with the ball, trying to get a shot off before time ran out. The 6th Man guys were counting down: "Ten, nine, eight, seven . . ." With only one or two seconds on the clock, the Spencerport guard still hadn't reached half court. He wasn't even at the center circle. But he heaved a last-second shot that almost went in. It hit the backboard in the perfect spot, and bounced into the rim and then right back out. If it didn't hit the backboard so hard, it would have gone in easy. It was almost one of those miracle shots you sometimes see on the local news.

I thought, *Man, that poor kid.* To come so close to hitting one of those last-second heaves, to getting on the local news. Also, it would have brought his team back to just ten points down, and they could have gone into halftime with their own momentum. I also thought, *That's something he'd remember his whole life, hitting a shot like that.* Then I thought it would have been pretty cool, to be in a game that was on the local news. Sure, I wanted us to win, and I wanted us to win big, but it was the kind of shot where you didn't really care about the score. On shots like that, you root for it to go in. As long as it didn't give them the lead, or cut too much into our lead, it would have been nice to see this Spencerport player sink it. It would have been something to remember, to be in the gym on Senior Night when a kid from the other team hit a half-court shot to end the first half. You don't see kids make shots like that too often.

Three

GROWING UP

THE THING ABOUT ME AND my brother was we were like twins. From the minute I started to really talk, that's how we were. We did everything together. Anyway, we spent all our time together. That was true even before I started talking, but now it was the two of us actually *being* together instead of just being in the same room together. Now we were like brothers, finally. Now we were like any other family. Josh was just a regular kid, and I guess that's all my parents ever wanted, for me to be a regular kid like my brother, so I did everything like Josh. Whatever he was into at the time, like baseball or basketball, that's what I was into. Bowling, too. We did that for a while, on Saturday mornings, I think. It was something I could do just as good as the other kids.

If I wasn't into it at first, my parents signed me up anyway and hoped I would catch on. This was something they did without talking to me or Josh about it, but after a while it was something me and Josh did on our own. It started out with organized sports and activities, and then it just continued from there.

DAVID McELWAIN

One of the first things we signed him up for was bumper bowling. Jason couldn't really do it, but we signed him up anyway. He was five or six years old, and I would walk him out on the lane and help him roll the ball down the alley. Otherwise he'd just stand there. He didn't really know what to do. All the other kids were throwing the ball and clapping and so forth, and Jason was just going through the process. He didn't really get it. That was hard for me, because the difference was so pronounced. And it was public, too. Everyone could see.

One time, he bolted. We were standing up at the line, and I used to hold on to his shirt to keep him from running off, but he got loose. I don't know why he took off, but he took off. Not straight down the alley, but across the other lanes, across the approaches. And I took off right after him, trying to grab him before he got killed by a bowling ball. Finally, I got him by the shirt and dragged him back.

People didn't understand about autism. They thought maybe Jason was just out of control. They thought he was like a problem kid, but he wasn't a problem kid. He couldn't help it. Even so, I was embarrassed. You know, you want your kid to be like everyone else. You sign him up for these activities, and then something like this happens and you see how different he really is.

When we were older, Josh had a big group of neighborhood friends, and they were always hanging out, and playing ball, and when I was about seven or eight years old, I started hanging out with them. That was just a year or two after I'd started talking, after I'd become a regular kid brother after all that time not talking and everything. Josh didn't mind. He said he liked having me around. Probably he did and he didn't, both.

All those years, with me just sitting in the corner, rocking back and forth or whatever I was doing, it's like I wasn't even there, so I guess he liked the company. I guess he was surprised that I was just a regular person inside. But at the same time I was different and I took a lot of attention, so maybe he didn't like it so much, at least not all the time. He went from being like an only child to being a big brother. His friends didn't mind having me around either, I don't think. They used to tease me about certain stuff, and play jokes on me, but it wasn't too bad. It was just regular big kid–little kid teasing, like they'd do to anyone's little brother. One of Josh's friends said I was like a mascot, which was a good way to put it. Some of Josh's friends, they had little brothers, too, and they treated their little brothers the same way, so it wasn't like they were picking on me because I was autistic. They were just picking on me because they were older. It was just the regular way they were with little brothers.

Once I started talking, once I started interacting with other people, Josh started to pay attention to me. Before that, I was just his autistic little brother. I was always around, that's all. He looked after me, like if we were in one room while my mother was in the kitchen getting dinner ready, but he didn't really play with me or anything. He didn't talk to me, or tease me, or even roughhouse with me. I wasn't really much fun to be around, I guess. But then I started talking and everything changed. Not overnight, because it's not like I said those first few words and all of a sudden I was talking, but gradually.

My personality changed—that's what everyone said. My relationship with my brother changed. After a couple months, I could talk in full sentences. I could say what I needed to say to make myself understood. My parents used to say it was much quieter around our house before I started to talk, and this was true, because I talked a lot. My mom continued pushing me to talk, and pushing me to talk, even after I said my first words. After my first words, I had to say my first sentences. I had to speak like all the other kids, like Josh. She wouldn't let me point at something as a way to ask for it, she'd pretend to ignore me until I actually said the words. If she asked what I did all day at school, I'd have to say what I did all day at school. I couldn't just say, "Nothing," or shrug my shoulders, like Josh probably did. She and my dad continued to read to me, a lot, because this was another good way to teach me how to talk, how to reach for the right words that would help me say exactly what I wanted to say.

DEBBIE McELWAIN

I was always reading about kids with autism, and in the literature it used to say how important it was to have an older sibling in the house, once the autistic child starts talking. It's one of the biggest things that helps the autistic child get out of his shell, so that was a big advantage for us, having the two boys so close in age. We were lucky.

Jason was always playing in the dining room, playing with his gum, and we were always dragging him out of the house, to whatever Josh was doing. Skiing lessons, tennis lessons, bowling... whatever it was, Jason would do it, too. At least he'd try. The violin, he didn't try. Josh started playing the violin and Jason wanted to play an instrument like his brother, so we started him on the drums. The violin was too difficult for him. Plus, he couldn't read music, so he just played the drums. It was the perfect instrument for him. It was just like banging those two packs of gum together, only with lessons.

The more Jason did, the more normal he seemed to his brother. Josh used to say he wanted to be a doctor so he could cure Jason. Then he'd say, "I hate his guts, but I want him normal." But no kid is normal in my book. There's no such thing. I don't like the word "normal," because people are just people. I don't like the word, but I catch myself using it all the time. I don't like the word "disability" either. That one I don't use. And I really don't like the word "retarded." That one I don't use, either. But these are the words Jason and Josh heard their whole lives, so what are you going to do?

I wasn't the most patient little kid—that's what I've been told. I've already written about this, but I'm writing about it again here because I think it needs repeating. If you told me something was gonna happen, I'd keep asking about it and asking about it until it finally happened. I couldn't wait. And you had better keep your word because I would call you on it—that's what my parents used to say. You probably had to have a lot of patience to be around me back then. You had to put up with a lot of my impatience. I didn't know how to wait for things to happen. I didn't know that sometimes people said things they didn't mean. Josh would say this made me seem like a real pain in the butt, which I guess I was. I didn't mean to be a pain in the butt, though. I just meant to stay on top of things, to get my questions answered right away, to be absolutely sure and clear about whatever was bothering me. Probably this had something to do with my mom being so precise with my language, with getting me to say exactly what I wanted, because it made me be really certain about certain things. That's one way to look at it, at least.

I don't think my parents ever left Josh alone in the house until he was maybe eleven or twelve years old, which meant I was maybe ten or eleven. I don't think they left me alone until I was much older, and when they finally did I had to call my mother at work all the time. I had to call when I let myself in after school, and I had to call if I wanted to go out to shoot hoops, or visit with my friend Brian down the street. When we were younger, when my mother had to work or do errands or something, we stayed with my grandmother. Sometimes we'd go to her house and sometimes she'd come over to our house. It depends. I was a handful—that's what everyone used to say—and my grandmother was one of the only people other than my mother and father who could handle me. That's what it means when you're a handful. There aren't a lot of people who can handle you.

There's a funny story we still talk about, from when I was maybe eight or nine. Josh and his friends, they still talk about it. They used to try to get me to do stuff when I was little, stuff I wasn't supposed to do. They'd give me a dollar and get me to do stuff. Or they'd just tell me to do it, and I'd do it. They'd do the same thing with the other little kids, I guess, only with me it was a little different. It wasn't dangerous stuff, or anything, because Josh looked after me and he was my brother and he was responsible for me, but it was stuff like using a lawn mower, which my mom didn't want me to do. That's what this story is about. I wasn't supposed to use anything mechanical, because I could get hurt. That's what everyone was worried about, so my mom wouldn't let me mow the lawn. All the other kids my age, they could mow their lawns, but not me. We were down the street, and it was summer, and Josh and his friends gave me a dollar to use a lawn mower, even though they knew I wasn't supposed to use a lawn mower. I didn't want to get into trouble, but I didn't want Josh and his friends to think I was a baby or anything, so I did what they said. Plus, I also wanted the dollar.

JOSH McELWAIN (brother)

Someone drove by and told my mother what Jason was doing, and she just flipped out. She was always flipping out about some of the stuff we used to do. But we were just kids, you know. So she grabbed a bike that was lying down by the curb in front of our house, a little kid's bike—I can't remember whose bike it was—and she hopped on and started pedaling down the street like a crazy person. You should have seen it! She was wearing this housecoat she used to wear, like a muumuu, and we could see her come flying down the street. It was windy, I guess, and her housecoat was just flapping all over the place, and she was yelling at us as she came down the street. She was yelling at us from like five or six houses away. She was really, really mad. And I've got to tell you, it was really, really embarrassing. My friends teased me about that for years and years, how she came riding down the street like the Wicked Witch of the West on that little kid's bicycle, hollering the whole way.

I got into a lot of trouble for that one. Jason, too. My parents punished him, too, because he should have known better. I felt bad about that, because of course me and my friends egged him on a little bit. Maybe he should have known better, but we talked him into it.

They played tricks on me, Josh and his friends. I didn't mind, because at least they were paying attention to me. At least I was part of the fun. I had some of my own friends, too. Brian Benson lived on our block, and he was one of my best friends growing up. He's still one of my best friends. He's two years younger, so we did a lot of sports together when we were little. We played T-ball together, because my parents thought it would be better if I played with the younger kids. I think you can start at five or six years old, so they waited until I was seven and signed me up with Brian. Also, we played in a summer children's golf league together. And Brian used to come with me and my dad and my brother up to a cottage my family had in the Thousand Islands in upstate New York. We would go boating and fishing and tubing. Josh usually brought one of his friends, too, and it would be a real guys' weekend. No women were allowed, although sometimes my grandmother came and helped with all the cooking and stuff. She liked having us around, she said. For a few years in a row, we went. It was like a tradition. It was like camp. We looked forward to it every year. My mother used to joke that it was a vacation for her, too, even though she stayed home. She said it was the only time she had any peace and quiet.

Me and my brother, we used to fight a lot. That's the thing I remember. Not serious, beating-each-other-up fighting, but fighting like brothers. Good fighting. Arguing. That's all. Mostly it was Josh teasing me and knowing how to get me upset about something. It was how we got along. One way this happened was we watched a lot of television together when we were little. Not regular television, because my parents didn't like us to watch regular television. But we watched a lot of videos. Disney movies, stuff like that. Some of these videos, we'd watch them over and over. It got so you could say a line from one of the movies and we'd know what line was coming next, but then after a while we stopped watching videos and started watching sports. That's the only regular television we watched. I think Josh was big into sports before me, and I followed because of him. After a while, whatever movies we were watching, whatever sports, we'd act out whatever was going on. If there was a fight, then we would fight. That's how it started, I think.

DAVID McELWAIN

Josh always gave it to Jason pretty good, especially when Jason was about ten and started to be real interested in sports. All of a sudden, he was addicted to watching sports and rooting for his favorite teams. He was a real bandwagon kid. His teams always won. He'd switch who he was rooting for every year, it seemed, just based on who had the better team, who had the best chance of winning. Whoever it was, Josh rooted for their rivals, just to get at Jason. He wasn't mean about it, but he liked to push Jason's buttons, that's all. It was like a good-natured rivalry. It wasn't mean.

So here's a story. When Shaquille O'Neal started playing for the Lakers, that was Jason's team, and Josh rooted for Sacramento, because they were always battling the Lakers. This was when the Lakers were winning all those championships. Every morning, the boys woke up and started to argue about their teams. You know how it is with boys. Whatever argument they were having when they went to bed, they'd pick up in the morning. Usually it was Josh who started it. Every morning, he'd find a way to get at Jason. He'd say, "Shaq got injured last night. He's out for the season." Just to tease him. Jason would come running in to me, all in tears, and he'd tell me what his brother told him. I'd tell Jason that Shaq didn't get injured. I'd tell him, "If he was injured, it would be in the paper."

Other kids would blow it off, but Jason wasn't able to. He wasn't able to shrug his shoulders and move on. He got real upset, and Josh liked that he got real upset, so he kept doing it. Every morning it was something else. The next morning after I told Jason it would be in the paper if Shaq got hurt, he came running in to me again, crying. He said, "Shaq got traded." I said, "Shaq did not get traded." He said, "It's in the paper! It's in the paper." So I go over and look at the paper, and Josh had written in the margin, in his own handwriting, that Shaq had been traded to Sacramento. I started laughing. I couldn't yell at Josh. I mean, he didn't even bother to type it up and make it look good—he just wrote it down in the margins of the sports page. And Jason fell for it.

I can still hear Jason yelling: "It's in the paper! It's in the paper!" And there in the corner was Josh, just laughing and laughing. So those kinds of things, yeah, they were like any two brothers, only Josh usually had the advantage.

I remember that Shaq story. Man, that really got me upset, the way Josh told me he was traded, but it wasn't so bad once my father explained everything to me. I believed it, and then I didn't believe it, and after that probably I wasn't even mad at Josh. I could see it was pretty funny, how he just tricked me and wrote in the margin of the newspaper. One of the things the magazine articles say about autism is that kids with autism don't have a sense of humor, but I don't think that's true with me. At least it's not true anymore. Maybe when I was little, when I wasn't talking, maybe then I didn't have a sense of humor. But now I think I do. Now I can laugh about stuff that happens to me. Now if I hear a good joke, I get it. I still get upset pretty easily, like I did about Shaq, but then once I calm down a little, I get it. I really do. I think about it and I get it and I can see that it's funny. I can even laugh about how upset I got, about how there was no reason to get upset after all. Like I said, that was a pretty funny move by Josh, to write in the margins like that, to make me think my favorite player was traded to his favorite team.

In the beginning, I didn't go to the same school as Josh. I went to a different school almost every year, all around Rochester, because I kept going to schools that had the best programs for kids like me. We were moved around according to placement and availability. My parents would sometimes ask to get me into a certain school, but in BOCES you had to go where there was room. I went to school in Spencerport, in Hilton, in Chili, in Churchville, in Kendall, and finally in Greece, which is the part of Rochester where I live. Some years, I had to sit on the bus for over an hour each way, in order to get to the school that was best for me. Churchville, that was the farthest away, and there were a lot of stops to get there. That's what I remember.

I don't think it's such a good thing, for a kid to move around to a new school every year. I think it was hard enough for me to make new friends just because I was autistic and because I was a handful, but it was even harder because each year I was in a new school with new kids. I think that's why some of my best friends were the regular kids I knew from our neighborhood, and the regular kids I knew because they were Josh's friends. By the end of each year, I had a lot of good friends in my special-ed classes, but then the school year would end and we wouldn't see each other anymore.

Every year, it was someplace new, but Greece is my home school district, so eventually that's where I went for good, but up until then it depended on which school had a one-to-six ratio of teachers to students. That's the program I had to have, because that's the program I was eligible for during my first few years of school. That's how you get a lot of attention, which I really needed, so each year my mom would talk to the board of education people and find out where they had that program. Wherever it was, that's where I'd go. After that, I was only eligible for the one-to-twelve program, which was still a good ratio for special ed. It was still a BOCES program for a while, only when I was thirteen years old it wasn't BOCES anymore. I was too old for the BOCES program I had been doing, which was one of the reasons I had to start going back to my home school district. In Greece, they had the special-ed classes I was eligible for in the same building as the regular kids, so I could see Josh and his friends, and my friends from the neighborhood, all during the day.

When I was little, I was only mainstreamed with the regular kids for gym class. That's what they call it when they put you with the regular kids, mainstreaming. I don't know how they came up with that word to describe special-ed kids going to school with regular kids. Someone explained it to me that it means we were all swimming up the same stream, the special-ed kids and the regular kids. It was the main stream, they said, but that didn't make any sense to me because we weren't swimming. We were going to school. If you ask me, they should just call it regular school, because that's what it is—it's us special-ed kids going to school with the regular kids.

Anyway, gym class was always my favorite part of the day. I was a good athlete and I liked sports and I liked being with the regular kids. I liked some of my classes, like art and woodshop. Some of the other classes, I didn't like so much. History and English, they had too much reading in them. I never really liked it when they had too much reading. Some of the teachers would make it easy for us, because they knew we weren't the best readers. I could listen in class to what it said in the books, but I didn't like to read. For lunch, I ate with the special-ed kids. A lot of them were my friends, so that worked out pretty good. A lot of them didn't talk or make eye contact or anything, but nobody really noticed or minded because we were all like that, in one way or another. Me and the other special-ed kids, we didn't go to each other's birthday parties or anything like that, but we were friends. I had my neighborhood friends and my brother's friends and then I had my friends in my special-ed class.

It turned out I was pretty good at sports. Josh was happy about that, because he was playing ball with me all the time. He was my first coach, in just about everything. All kinds of ball, that's what we played. I wanted to be just like him, but then sometimes I'd get better than him and he'd quit. Like with cross-country. He was on the team first, and then I came along and he knew I could beat him, so he quit. He didn't say that's why he quit, but that's what I think. I'll tell more about that later. And basketball. Josh played in our local league, and then he tried out for the school team and didn't make it, so he didn't play so much anymore after that, but I kept playing. I'll tell more about that, too, but for now I'll just say that I played basketball all the way through my senior year, and the whole time I thought about Josh because he was the one who taught me how to shoot.

The first sport I really tried was baseball. My dad says it was bowling or maybe swimming, but those aren't really team sports. Baseball is a team sport, and it's hard for an autistic kid to be in a team sport. It's hard for the kid, and it's hard for the coach, and it's hard for the other players, that's what everybody says, but I think the only reason it was hard for me and my situation was because nobody knew what to expect. That's all. Nobody knew if I would have an autistic outburst, or if they had to treat me differently, or make it easy for me, or what. But they didn't have to do any of those things. They just had to treat me like a regular player and I would do fine. That's what we figured out along the way.

I was never the best kid on the team and I was never the worst kid on the team. It didn't really matter what sport it was, I was always somewhere in the middle. Like baseball. I had the same Little League coach for five years, and we always won the pennant. His name was Jim Depasquale. First it was T-ball, when I was seven, and then it was hardball, up until I was about thirteen or fourteen. I don't know why, but Coach Depasquale always picked me for his team. Maybe he thought I was his good-luck charm because we always won. But I think we won because he was a good coach. He always told the players on his team that they had to be a hitter. He didn't like it when kids stood at the plate with their bats on their shoulders. He wanted us to swing at the ball. He didn't have to tell me, though, because I swung at everything. That's what I remember.

DAVID McELWAIN

Jason's right about that. You could strike him out every time. All you had to do was throw him three pitches he couldn't reach and he'd swing at every single one of them. That's the way he was. But he was a joy to watch, for me. Everybody liked him. He was a real charmer, even then. The other parents, they'd root for him like they were rooting for their own kids. Everyone wanted him to do well. And I could sit in the stands with my mother and father, or my in-laws, and think he was like every other kid out there on the field. Really, you could watch him play and think he was no different.

My thing was, at the beginning of a new season, with a new coach, I never wanted to tell anyone he was autistic. I wanted Jason to make his own first impression. My wife, that'd be the first thing she'd do. She'd call the coach right away and talk to him about autism, but I didn't want Jason to be treated differently. I didn't want the coach to be afraid to put him into the game. He could play just like any other kid could play, but he was also autistic.

My parents didn't really argue a lot when I was little, but this was one of the few things they disagreed about, whether or not to tell people I was autistic. Usually if they disagreed, and it was something to do with me and autism, they did things how my mom wanted. Or a better way to put it is my mom just did things how she wanted and my dad followed. My dad, he wanted to just sign me up for whatever it was and see how I could do. My mom, she had to think about it and read about it and talk to people about it before she'd sign me up for anything. She had very strong ideas about how to deal with my autism. She was the one who did all the reading and took me to all my doctors and everything. She was the one who talked to all the therapists and tried all the different treatments that people thought could help. She saw something once on television that said some patients with autism had a kind of growth in their brain, like a tumor. It said the growth could be removed. So the next day she made an appointment for me to be tested at Strong Memorial, which is the big hospital in Rochester. That's where I had all those tests, when I was little. One of my doctors, Dr. Salkas, was at Strong Memorial. He was an autism specialist. So we went to the appointment, and I had to be asleep for the test, but it turned out the thing they were talking about didn't apply to me. What I had, they couldn't just remove with an operation. So I left the hospital and I still had autism.

With my teachers, my father never said anything. He just left it to my mother to do it how she wanted. The word for how my father was about school is "easygoing." But my mom was different. For example, when my doctor and my teachers wanted me to try a certain medicine to help me concentrate, my mom didn't want me to take it because she thought it was a crutch. That was always the word she used for something that was supposed to make things easy, a "crutch." She thought if I could overcome my autism by myself, without any medicine, it would stay overcome. She thought if I used medicine to overcome it, it would just come back when I stopped taking the medicine. This was how she explained it to me.

For another example, my mother would never help me with my homework because that would be a crutch, and also because she thought if she did help me the teacher would never know what kind of work I could do on my own. She'd make sure I understood the assignment, but then she left me alone. She said if I got it wrong, the teacher would fix it with me and explain it to me better, and then after that happened she would go over it with me at home. I thought that was a good strategy. I don't know if my dad agreed with her idea about this or not, but I couldn't ask him for help with my homework because he'd say, "Mom doesn't think we should help you with your homework." It was the same way with Josh. They wouldn't help him either, and he was just a regular kid. They wouldn't even let him use a calculator for math, and everybody uses a calculator for math. But like I said, my mother doesn't like us to have a crutch, and now she says Josh is majoring in math at college and studying to be a math teacher and it's because he never used a calculator when he was little.

When I started playing sports, my mother always talked to the coach beforehand, even though my father didn't want her to. When I was older, I didn't want her to either. It's not that I was embarrassed or anything. It's just that I wanted to be treated like the regular kids. When I was younger, I don't think I knew about it. Usually she'd just introduce herself to the coach and tell how I had autism and how I might need some help. When I got to middle school, I went out for the cross-country team and she told the coach I couldn't tie my shoes, and then she arranged it so that I had a guardian angel to help me tie my shoes before every race and practice. It was just another kid on the team who could tie shoes, but she called him a guardian angel. That's the name they had for it in the athletic department.

DEBBIE McELWAIN

Of course I had to tell the coach. What else could I do? How else would he know how to handle Jason, unless he knew he was apt to throw an autistic outburst if he didn't play well? The coach had to know. Dave always said, "Why does he have to know?" And I always said, "If we're not there, what will happen if something happens?"

Dave's thing was, we had to be there all the time. If one of us couldn't make it, we'd make sure Dave's parents were there, or my parents. That's just how it had to be. Every game, every practice, every clinic, whatever Jason was doing, one of us was there, all the way from six or seven years old when he started up until middle school, when he started playing for these school teams. After that we thought he could handle it on his own, because he could basically control his outbursts by that point, and because he was playing in a school setting. It wasn't like Little League, or GBA youth basketball, where it's just parent volunteers doing the coaching. These were teachers, trained professionals, so they could deal with Jason if something came up.

It wasn't just for tying shoes, me having a guardian angel on the team. It was for a lot of things. Even though they called it a guardian angel, it was really just my friend. It could be a different friend each time. It depended on who was there to help me, who was running in the same event or working on the same things in practice. And whoever it was, they were happy to help me tie my shoes, and tell me to follow the trail, and remind me to drink lots of water if it was a really hot day. That's how it is with friends, you help each other out. Sometimes, I would help them with certain stuff. You don't need the school or the coach or your mom to get involved. You just do it. That's the great thing about team sports. It means you have teammates, and teammates help each other out, even for silly things like tying your shoes.

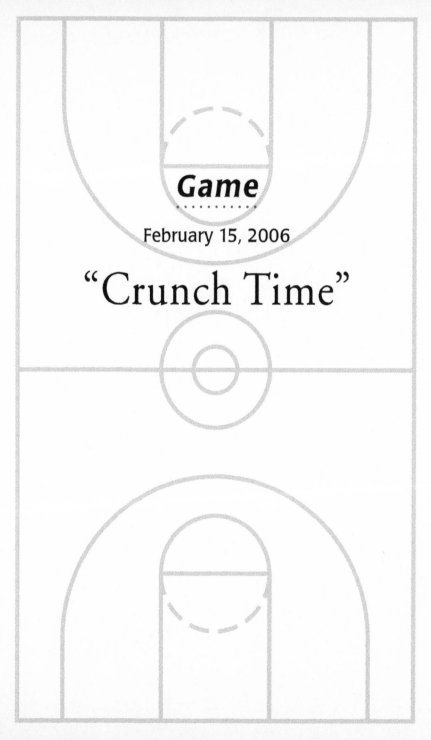

Game

February 15, 2006

"Crunch Time"

USUALLY AT HALFTIME, COACH JOHNSON took us back to the locker room to talk about the game. We didn't have the nicest locker rooms at Greece Athena, so sometimes we'd go to a classroom and have our halftime meeting there. I'm not writing this to say something bad about Greece Athena, which is a really great school, but there was more room for the players to sit in the classroom, and it didn't smell so bad. So that's what we did for the Spencerport game. We just went to the nearest classroom and sat around and talked about the game, how important it was for us to keep focused, what was going on in that other game we couldn't control. The weird thing about it was that when you go into the locker room, there are no other people around. You go into the locker room and it's just you and your teammates. It's closed off to everyone else. Out in the classroom, though, there are other people around. There are kids in the hallways, people standing around, people looking through the window of the door to the classroom.

I knew what Coach was going to say before we even sat down. That's how it is with a good coach like Coach Johnson. You play for him for a couple years, you start to know how he thinks, what he wants to see from you on the court, what he wants from the guys on the bench. Basically he liked how we were playing, but he didn't like the scoreboard. I could have told you that. All of the players could have told you that. We had a nice lead, but we weren't up big. We weren't putting Spencerport away. Coach said the score didn't really show how the game was going. It didn't show how we were capable of playing. I guess I was starting to think like a coach, after all that time on the bench, helping out, because I was thinking the same thing. Some games are like that, in basketball. You can take another team out of its game and still not put them away. That's why basketball is such a great game, because you just never know. On paper, you can have a team beat. You can even beat them up and down the court. But on the scoreboard, the other team can hit a couple key shots and make a couple key stops and still stay in the game. If they keep it close, anything can happen.

It was my first halftime talk as a varsity player, and I was listening and not listening, all at the same time. I was thinking about what would happen once I got into the game. I was hoping I'd have a chance to score, to contribute. I liked the way it felt like Coach was talking to me. This was the part when I was listening. All the other halftime talks, there wasn't anything I could do about whatever Coach was saying, but this time I could take what he was saying and do something about it in the game. Most of the guys, they weren't too worried about winning the game. Even Coach wasn't too worried—I don't think. But these were the things he had to say to keep the team focused. These were the things we had to cover.

I liked also that it would soon be my turn to get into the game. There were only sixteen minutes left, so if Coach was planning to put me in he would have to do it soon. This was the part when I wasn't listening. This was the part that couldn't wait for the rest of the game to happen. I was daydreaming. I was thinking what it would be like when the public-address guy said my name and the people went crazy. I knew they'd go crazy. They were going crazy already, and I hadn't even gotten in yet.

We went back out for the halftime shootaround and this time it felt like there were even more people in the gym. I'll tell you what: it was pretty packed before the game started, but now it was really, really packed. I guess more of the parents had come in since the game started, after getting back from work. Probably there were more Spencerport parents, too, because they didn't need to be there early for the Senior Night ceremony. So the people just kept coming as the first half went on, and now both sides of the gym were mostly full.

I tried to get in a good warm-up. I wanted to be ready. I took a lot of shots, mostly from behind the three-point line. I don't know why I was mostly shooting threes, but I grabbed a lot of long rebounds and I just put the ball back up from wherever I was standing. In between shots, I'd stop and talk to some of my friends in the stands. I know you're not supposed to talk to the people in the stands when you're warming up, but I couldn't help it. I'm a friendly person. If people talk to me, I talk to them. The 6th Man kids, with their yellow shirts, they kind of spilled onto the floor during halftime, and everyone was all loose and talking and congratulating me. I hadn't done anything yet except sit next to the coaches on the bench, but already they were congratulating me and it felt good that they were congratulating me. They were saying, "Way to go, J-Mac!" And, "Good luck!" "Go get 'em!" Things like that. A couple of pretty girls said "Hey" to me, as I was shooting, and I liked that. Usually, I wasn't shy around girls, but I wasn't around them so much that I didn't like it when they said "Hey" to me, so I said "Hey" back and kept shooting.

We took the ball to start the second half, and Rickey Wallace got us started with a jumper from the top of the key on our first possession, putting us up 30–15 and doubling up Spencerport for the first time since midway through the second quarter. I thought, *Okay, this is a good start. This is a statement.* Then, on the very next Spencerport possession, we stole the ball and had a fast break for an easy layup, and as we were pushing down the court I was thinking we were about to put the game away, but we missed the shot. It's opportunities like that that give the other team a chance to think they're still in the game—that's what Coach always said—but Spencerport turned it over again and this time down the floor one of our guys was fouled. It's like we kept giving Spencerport a chance to stay in the game, and they kept giving it back. Like we didn't want to take control, and they didn't either. Do you know that game called hot potato? That's where you keep passing the potato around and you don't want to get stuck holding the potato when time is called. That's what this game was like, in a lot of ways. Like nobody wanted to take control.

We hit the first free throw and missed the second, and then Spencerport answered with an easy layup on their end of the floor. We came right back after that with an easy layup of our own, and the Spencerport coach called a thirty-second time-out, to get his players to focus. It was a good time-out, I thought, because it came about two or three minutes into the third quarter and Greece Athena had been dominating the play. If I was the Spencerport coach, I would have called a time-out, too, because things were definitely starting to go our way. As a coach, you want to stop that kind of momentum before it has a chance to really start. As a player on the bench, you want it to keep going and going until there's nothing left for the guys on the floor to prove and they start getting the reserves into the game.

During the time-out, the public-address guy announced the winning number for a 50/50 raffle being run by our booster club. The winning ticket was worth $204. I wondered if maybe my parents had bought a ticket. They usually did, when they had those kinds of fund-raisers at my school. The winning ticket number was 468971. Nobody moved to the scorer's table to claim their prize, and nobody shouted out that they had the winning number. That's what I would have done, if I had the winning number. I would have jumped up and down and screamed, because $204 is a lot of money. Probably the person with the winning number wasn't in the gym, because you had to be in the gym in order to win, and I couldn't see anybody jumping up and down and screaming. Probably my parents hadn't won, either, because they were in the gym and I could see they hadn't moved toward the scorer's table or anything. I could see they weren't jumping up and down and screaming. This was the kind of stuff I was thinking about during the time-out. I should have been listening to Coach, because maybe he was going to put me into the game, but instead I was thinking about this 50/50 raffle.

We came out of the time-out and went straight into our half-court press, which Coach always liked us to play to keep the pressure on the other team. Like I said, this was one of his big things, and it works best when you're scoring because you have a chance to pressure the other team on their inbounds play. When it's just off a rebound or a loose ball, it's not really a half-court press. It's just good defense. Anyway, the Spencerport guard rushed a shot from behind the three-point line, and we grabbed the rebound and pushed down the floor, where a frustrated Rangers player was called for a foul. This time, we sank both shots, which meant we could go back into our half-court press on the inbounds play.

That's pretty much how the game went, for the first few minutes of the third quarter. Back and forth, but mostly our way. We were keeping the pressure on, we were controlling the pace, but we weren't pulling away on the scoreboard. In fact, we missed a bunch of shots, and Spencerport broke us down a couple times on the other end of the floor for easy layups and put backs, and at one point I looked up and the score was 39–24. This was still a commanding lead, but we were only up 11–9 in the third quarter. Obviously, this wasn't the way Coach wanted us to start the second half, so he called a time-out. This was another good time-out, I thought, because it was a good time to get us to pause and think about how the game was going before it went in some direction we didn't want it to. That's the thing about time-outs. Unless it's at the end of the game and you're talking about a last-second shot or something, it's not usually a time to talk about a specific strategy or a set play. Sometimes it is, but usually it's not. Usually it's a time to get your team to take a deep breath and think about what's happening on the court. It's a time to get focused and to talk generally about the game and not specifically about a particular play or anything, so that's why this was another good time-out.

Also, during this time-out, I learned that the person who had the winning 50/50 raffle ticket wasn't in the gym, because the public-address guy came on and said he was pulling another number and that this time the prize would only be $102. This time the winning number was different, and the announcer called it out twice because nobody responded when he said it the first time. I thought maybe this meant this second person wasn't in the gym either and they would never give away the prize money. I don't know why I worried so much about the raffle, but I guess it just got stuck in my head.

My friend Levar Goff came out of the time-out and did a nice stutter-step move off the dribble from the top of the key and drove the lane for an easy layup. Then Spencerport turned the ball over and we really started pressuring the boards on our offensive end. We missed a couple shots, but we kept getting the rebound, and eventually one of our guys went up for an easy put back and was fouled. The momentum was really starting to turn, just on these first few possessions coming out of our last time-out, and then we stole the ball again and one of our guys hit a three-pointer, and the next thing I knew we were up 48–24, which meant we'd gone on a 9–0 run since Coach called that time-out. That's all you need to know about whether or not it was a good time-out, right? When you go on a 9–0 run, it means it was a good time-out.

This was the first time in the second half that I started hearing chants of "J-Mac!" coming from the 6th Man section. They said it all kinds of ways. They stretched it out, like before:

"Jayyyy-Mac! Jayyyy-Mac!" They said it over and over, with clapping: "J-Mac!" *Clap, clap.* "J-Mac!" *Clap, clap.* There was less than a minute to go in the quarter, and they kept it up, louder and louder each time down the court. I wondered if there was one kid in charge of the cheering, or if people just said whatever they felt like saying and hoped other people would join them. However it worked, the 6th Man kids switched to just saying "J-Mac!" over and over, without any clapping or stretching it out, and soon it started to reach around the whole gymnasium, like the wave you see people doing at football and baseball stadiums.

A lot of kids would have been embarrassed to hear their name like that, but not me. I liked it, but I didn't want Coach Johnson to think I'd asked everyone to call out my name. Over and over, they kept chanting my name. Louder and louder. We were still playing, our guys were out there hustling, trying to push the lead before time ran out in the fourth quarter, but I don't think too many people in the stands were watching the game. They were, but they weren't. They were too busy cheering and chanting and clapping to pay good attention to what was going on down on the floor. What was going on was Spencerport was playing like their season depended on cutting our lead. They kept missing their shots, but they were fighting for the offensive rebounds and coming up with the ball. Coach Johnson couldn't have been too happy about it. At one point, one of our guys finally came down with the defensive rebound, but then one of the Spencerport players stripped him of the ball. But then we stole it right back and managed to push it down to our end of the court, where Levar Goff tapped in an offensive rebound to put us up 50–24 to end the quarter. That meant we were on an 11–0 run since Coach Johnson's last time-out, and now everyone was all pumped and excited. The whole gym started chanting, "We want J-Mac! We want J-Mac!"

The public-address guy came on again and announced that no one had claimed the 50/50 prize, but I don't think too many people heard him. There was too much cheering and chanting and clapping for anyone to hear much of anything except, "We want J-Mac! We want J-Mac!" Over and over. Louder and louder. The pretty girls from before, at halftime, they were right down there with the 6th Man kids, calling out my name.

It was pretty cool. I'll tell you that.

Four

GREECE ATHENA

I WAS REALLY PSYCHED TO go to middle school and high school. Most kids, they don't get too psyched about school, but I wasn't like most kids about school. I liked all the noise and activity of school. I liked the social part of school. I didn't care too much about the actual school part, but I didn't mind it too much either, and I liked seeing all my friends and having someplace exciting to go to each day. Otherwise, it can get pretty boring, just hanging around the house and waiting for the other kids on my block to get home from whatever they were doing. I also liked learning some of the stuff I learned in my classes. I liked subjects like math. I didn't like to read too much, but I liked if they could tell me about it in class.

My parents were psyched about me going to middle school and high school, too. This is what they tell me now, but it's also what they told me back then. Since I was little, they were worried I would never go to school with the regular kids in my neighborhood. That was one of their biggest concerns. They worried they would have to keep finding some new BOCES program for me every year. They worried I would be so many places I wouldn't fit in anywhere, or that I'd spend so much time back and forth on the special bus I had to take to get to a school that was far away from my house, or that the regular kids wouldn't want to have anything to do with me. My mom was really upset about this. She tells me now she used to go into her room to have a good cry about it. I don't remember that.

As I got older, as I got more and more involved with sports and my brother and his friends, I became more and more social. I think this helped with my autism, me being involved in sports and being more social. Every year when I went in for my physical, Dr. Vora used to tell my mom he was surprised by my development, by how well I was doing, because as a kid I had been diagnosed as severely autistic, but when I got to be ten and twelve and fourteen, it wasn't so severe anymore. It was more mild. So that's what I mean when I say it probably helped with my autism. Probably I could never read or write or think about things the same way as the other kids, but I was able to do a lot more than anyone ever thought, and now here I was ready to go to school with the regular kids in my neighborhood.

We go to Greece Athena, which is one of four high schools in Greece, which is the suburb where we live in Rochester. The others are Greece Arcadia, Greece Olympia, and Greece Odyssey, and you have to go to one of those depending on where you live. The team names are the Trojans, the Titans, the Spartans, and the Leopards. The names are all supposed to make you think of ancient Greece, because of the name of our town, but that's not why I was psyched to go. I was psyched because at Athena the middle school is attached to the high school, and I knew some of the kids, and Josh was a year ahead of me and I knew all of his friends, and I would finally stop moving from school to school every year. I didn't like that, when I was little. I was like my parents about this. I didn't like how every year I had to start school in a new place, and meet new kids and new teachers, because I like it when things are familiar. I like it when things are a certain way. In all the books and articles about autism, it says autistic kids like to have a routine, and that's true for me, too. Probably it's true for everyone. Probably it doesn't matter if you're autistic. It's just better if you know what to expect.

So I went to Greece Athena knowing what to expect, a little bit. Of course, I didn't really know exactly how it would be, but I knew the building, and I knew the routine, and I knew a lot of the kids and the teachers and the coaches, so I wasn't too worried about any of that. Actually, I wasn't too worried about anything, although my parents were worried. They thought maybe they made a mistake, putting me in with my regular grade with regular kids my age. They didn't talk to me about this at the time, because if they did I would have said it wasn't a mistake, but they were allowed to keep me in an elementary or middle school setting for another few years, because of my disability. In the BOCES program, in New York, I could go to high school until I was twenty-one, but who wants to go to high school until you're twenty-one?

DAVID McELWAIN

What Jason's talking about is our decision to place him back in our home school district, with kids his own age. He'd been going to school in Hilton, where the elementary schools go from kindergarten to sixth grade, but in Athena they go from kindergarten to fifth grade. He'd just finished his sixth-grade year, so we moved him to Athena Middle School as a seventh-grader. He was classified as a seventh-grader, but we could have had him classified as a sixth-grader. He has an October birthday, so that made him one of the younger kids, and a kid like Jason, he doesn't have to be one of the younger kids in his grade. We could have put him in as a sixth-grader, and he would have been one of the older kids by just a month or two, and nobody would have known the difference. Jason would never have known the difference, because he was starting school with these kids for the first time. Sixth grade, seventh grade, it wouldn't have mattered.

We didn't think about this too much at the time. My wife and I were just so pleased to see Jason moving on to middle school, to be going from class to class like all the other kids, to be using the special locker they had for him there. He couldn't work the combination locks they had, so they set him up with a special lock with a key and he was able to manage that just fine. It was only later that we came to regret it. It was only when Jason's friends were graduating and moving on and we were worrying what Jason was going to do next that we realized he could have been in school for another year or two. That's when we started to think we'd made a bad decision. We talked about it with Jason during his senior year, but he didn't want to stay in school. He didn't want to be a "supersenior." That's the term they have for the kids who have to repeat their senior year, and it has a negative connotation to it, but in Jason's case it wouldn't have been a negative. It would have been a positive. He could have had an extra year, because with a kid like Jason you worry how he'll do outside of school. You worry if he can hold down a job, things like that. So keeping him back that one year, it would have saved us all a lot of worry.

No way was I going to be a supersenior. That's the name they have for it, and it makes it sound better than it is. It's a good thing my parents didn't push that because I would have pushed right back. I mean, I was already a senior. I was going to all my classes and doing all my work. My teachers all liked me. Plus, all the other seniors on the basketball team were graduating, so it's not like I could come back and play another year on varsity. I'd already had my Senior Night and everything, and you shouldn't get to do that stuff twice, right? But I don't want to write too much about my senior year right away, because first I want to tell how things were when I started school in Greece. In Greece, the special-ed kids were mixed in with the regular kids for gym and lunch. There were also other regular classes you could take, like music and art and woodshop. All the other subjects like math and reading were just with the special-ed kids, so the good thing was I could see my friends during the day. You moved from class to class, just like the regular kids. I could see Josh and his friends during the day. I could see them at lunch. I could see them at gym. I could see them in the hallways as we moved around between periods. I still wasn't what they called a mainstreamed kid, but I was a lot closer to being a mainstreamed kid than I was in Hilton, which was the last place I went to school. For a lot of the day I was just like everyone else.

The biggest difference was now I could go out for school sports, which was something I always wanted to do, so I went out for the cross-country team right then in my first season. It was the fall season of my seventh-grade year. They didn't have any cuts on the cross-country team, but even if they did, I think I would have made it. I was a good runner. I was fast. The only thing I couldn't do was tie my shoes, which my mom already talked about. Also, I didn't know how to run the right way. I was just fast on my own, because nobody ever taught me how to run fast in a race, so I had to learn all of that stuff, too. I had to learn to stop moving my arms so much when I ran, and to lean forward a little, and to pace myself, and to stay straight. It's hard to stay straight in cross-country, because you're running through the woods or in an open field. In track, there are lines for you to follow, but in cross-country there are no lines, so that was one of the things I had to learn, how to follow the lines when there weren't any lines. One of the tricks I learned was to follow the runner in front of you, but sometimes I was the one in front, so that didn't always work.

Josh used to run on the school team, too, but he stopped when he saw how fast I was. He didn't want to be the second-fastest runner in the family. He didn't like losing to me. We were always very competitive, me and Josh. When I was little, I could never beat him at anything, but then when I got older I got a little better at some things, like running. Later on, I think I got better at basketball, too. He taught me how to shoot, and then one day I could shoot better than him. I think that was because I worked at it more. I practiced and practiced.

Anyway, I really liked being on the cross-country team. I liked going every day after school to practice. I liked the meets, too, running in those races with all those other kids from all those other schools. I was on the track team, too. That's what they play in the spring. I didn't make the basketball team, though. On the basketball team, they had cuts. There were a ton of kids who went out for the middle school team, and they only took fifteen. I was disappointed, but I kept playing basketball. I kept practicing. My mom was probably more disappointed than I was, because she didn't understand about high school sports and cuts. I understood, so I didn't mind so much. My dad understood, too, because he knew about sports and how things were on teams where there were cuts. Josh got cut when he went out for the seventh- and eighth-grade basketball team, so my mom knew it happened to the regular kids, too. He also got cut when he went out for junior varsity basketball, so then he started playing tennis and he got really good at that instead, and by then I think my mom understood. When I got cut that first time, she just thought if you wanted to play you should be allowed to play, but everyone knows that there are a lot of good players, and sometimes a coach sees something in one player he doesn't see in you.

I still had my dream of playing basketball on the high school team and winning a sectional title. I don't know where that dream came from, or when I started talking about it, but it was always there, for as long as I can remember. I told myself the coach could cut me from the team but he couldn't cut me from my dream. That's the way I looked at it. You know, Michael Jordan got cut from his high school team the first time he tried out, so the thing you have to do is never give up. Probably this was one of the first times I had to talk myself up like that, after I got cut from the middle school basketball team. I thought, *I have to*

keep playing, I have to keep trying, so I kept playing in the Greece
Basketball Association league. That's the name for the local GBA
league I'd always played in, since I was little. Josh played in it,
too. A lot of our friends did. Even the kids who made the middle
school team kept playing GBA, because our games were on the
weekends, so there was some good basketball there.

JIM JOHNSON

Jason was coming out to these clinics we ran when he
was still in middle school. It was a way for us to identify
the kids coming up, but it was also a way to keep basketball a priority for these kids, so we ran a year-round program. We had open gym time. We had a town camp we
ran every year. The weight room was always open. And
by the end of middle school Jason was coming to these
camps, and you could see he had a tremendous amount
of passion and enthusiasm for the game. He was a little
on the small side, and he was maybe a step or two on the
slow side, but he was a hard worker. You could see there
was something there.

I want to write for a while about how it was with the other
kids in school. I'll write more about the basketball stuff after, but
for now I want to tell about my friends. I had a lot of friends,
more than I could count. A lot of times, I hear stories being told
about me that say I was teased a lot in high school. That's true,
but it's only partly true. I told about it before, a little bit, but I'll
tell about it again. Sometimes, the other kids would tease me,
but usually I was in on the joke, and when I wasn't it was never

so bad. It was mostly the good kind of teasing. I never minded it, because these kids were my friends. They didn't mean anything by it. Plus, I liked that they were paying attention to me. I liked that everyone knew who I was. I liked that I fit in.

The special-ed kids, they wouldn't tease me. We were always nice to each other. It was the regular kids who did the teasing, because that's what regular kids do. Sometimes at lunch I sat with my friends from the neighborhood, like Brian Benson. Or I sat with Josh and his friends, if we had lunch scheduled for the same period. And what happens, when you sit in the cafeteria all the time with the regular kids, there's a lot of teasing. The regular kids were always teasing each other, and once in a while it was just my turn to get teased, that's all. It wasn't really a big deal. My mom would hear stories about what happened in school during the day, and she'd decide that these weren't good kids, that they were picking on me because I was autistic, and we had to tell her it wasn't really like that. Me and Josh, we had to tell her it was just normal teasing.

STEVE KERR (high school friend, Greece Athena teammate)

There was one time, we were in the locker room. I think it was after a j.v. practice. And somebody got the idea to stuff Jason in one of the lockers. It wasn't because he was autistic or anything, but he was little. That was really the only reason. He was probably one of the smallest kids on the team, so they tried to stuff him in a locker. I don't think anyone else would have fit. We were just a bunch of stupid kids, and this was the kind of stupid stuff we'd do. Jason actually thought it was funny. We all

thought it was funny. Nobody was out to hurt him or anything. Nobody was trying to take advantage. And the interesting thing is, after the first time it happened, Jason
was always trying to get us to stuff him in the locker
again.

There was another time, after practice, when some of the guys
folded me up in the bleachers. You know how you can push the
bleachers into the wall, and how all the benches fit together like
a puzzle? Well, the bottom bench has a kind of flap on it, and
you can lift it up and crawl inside. That's what they did with me.
They didn't force me in or anything, but they were cheering me
on and telling me to do it. I don't know whose idea it was, but
everyone thought it would be funny. I thought it would be funny,
too, only when they closed me in and folded up the bleachers, I
couldn't get out by myself. They shut off the lights in the gym
and closed the door, and a part of me knew they weren't really
gonna leave me there like that, but there was another part that
thought maybe they would.

JOSH McELWAIN

My mom always thought the kids were bullying Jason,
but it wasn't like that. Jason would tell her what happened. Not like he was ratting people out or anything,
but like he just wanted to share what happened to him
that day. And she'd get really mad, but it was just good-
natured stuff, just playing around. At home, I would tease
the crap out of him, but that was just me and him. When
we were at school, I tried to look after him. That doesn't

mean I stepped in every time the guys were goofing around with him, but if something looked like it was getting out of hand, I said something. That didn't happen too much, though. Once in a while, yeah, I guess things got a little out of hand, but no one was ever cruel or hurtful or anything. It was never a big deal.

By freshman year, I had a ton of friends. I knew a lot of the girls, too. Everyone used to smile at me in the halls, or wave hello. I didn't hang out with the regular kids too much after school, but in school I was like one of the guys. All the teachers liked me, too. When I was older, when I got a cell phone, I filled it up with everyone's phone number. I had over a hundred numbers in just a couple weeks. I'd walk up to people I knew and ask them if I could put their number in my phone. They'd give me their number and I'd give them mine, and after that we were friends. After that we would call each other sometimes.

Once in a while, I'd get invited to one of their parties. On Friday nights and Saturday nights, there were usually parties. I went, but some of these parties, like open-house parties, were really loud and crowded. I didn't like it when things were loud and crowded. I liked going to other kinds of parties instead. Freshman year, on the cross-country team, we used to have pasta parties on Friday nights before our Saturday meets. One of the seniors would usually have the party, and we would all go. I don't think I missed a single one of these pasta parties. All the parents knew me because I loved to eat. When my dad came to pick me up, they'd say they didn't know where I put all the pasta, because I ate so much and I was still so skinny.

Basically, I wanted to be just like the other high school kids. Me and my neighborhood friends, we'd hang out at each other's houses sometimes, or we'd shoot hoops, or play some kind of ball. There was always something to do, and some regular kids to do it with. It just didn't have to be at those loud, crowded parties.

That gives a good idea how it was with the other kids in school, how I fit in, so now I can go back to basketball and tell that part of the story. I kept trying out for the school team every year. Eighth grade, for the middle school team. Ninth grade, for the freshman team. And I kept getting cut. I tried to be positive about it. My dad and my brother helped me with this. Like I said, there were a lot of kids going out for these teams, and there were a lot of good players. I kept going to Coach Johnson's camps and clinics, and I started to know a lot of the coaches. I was always hanging around the gym after school, or on school vacations. In basketball, they have a word for a kid like that who always hangs around the gym. They call him a gym rat, so I guess that's what you could have called me.

That's one of the reasons why Coach Amoroso asked me to be the team manager of the junior varsity, after I didn't make the team. He knew how committed I was to basketball and to the team. He knew how important it was to me. Also, he knew I was friends with a lot of the players and that I'd work really hard for him. He talked to Coach Johnson about it first. He wanted to know if he thought it was a good idea, and Coach Johnson agreed that it was a good idea, and then I agreed too. It was such a good idea I wished I'd thought of it. My mom and dad also thought it was a good idea. In fact, my mom had already called Coach Amoroso before I got cut from the team, and discussed the possibility of me being manager and what my duties would be. She always has a lot of questions. She had wanted to know if I would be treated like a regular part of the team, and he said yes. He said as far as he was concerned, I was just like his other players, only I wouldn't really get to play. I could help him out in practice. I could rebound for the other players when they were practicing their foul shots. I could help set up drills. I could get water and towels and whatever else anybody needed. I could help the other team's manager put our team's names in their score book, and do other pregame stuff. That would be my role. I would be a member of the team, only I wouldn't be one of the players.

I said, "Yes, sure, I'd love to be the team manager." And then I remembered how my mom always said to be polite, so I said, "Thank you for asking me."

I really liked being the team manager. I still got to play a lot of basketball during our practices. I still hung around the gym all the time after school, and got in my shooting practice. I got to go to our away games, too. I had to wear a shirt and tie. This was when I started thinking that the white shirt and black clip-on tie I wore were good luck. Later on, when I was managing the varsity team and we were on a winning streak, I didn't change the color of my shirt or tie, but if we lost a game I changed it and tried some new colors. I was superstitious about how we were doing, and I tried to keep our good luck going however I could.

And then at the end of the junior varsity season, Coach Amoroso said he had a surprise for me. He said, "How would you like to dress in uniform for our last game?"

I said, "Yes, sir. I would like that very much. Thank you." I wasn't expecting to be able to dress for the game, so this really was a surprise.

Coach Amoroso said he couldn't promise me that I would get into the game, but he promised he would try to get me in. He said if the right situation came up, if it made good basketball sense, he would get me in. He gave me a jersey. It was a number 22 jersey. It was the same number my cousin wore for the Spencerport football team, so I thought that was cool. I didn't ask for it or anything, but it matched up with a number from someone in my family, so I thought it was like my legacy to wear that number. It didn't really fit, but I didn't care. It was a high school basketball jersey. It was *my* high school basketball jersey. And it was my cousin's number. That was all I cared about.

Before Coach Amoroso gave me the jersey, he talked to Coach Johnson about it, and then Coach Johnson had to clear it with our athletic director. His name was Randy Hutto, and it turned out he also had a kid who was autistic, so of course he said it would be okay. I mean, he would have probably said it was okay anyway, because I was just a regular student and it was just a regular basketball game and it wasn't hurting anybody if I played, but Mr. Hutto said he was happy to help me reach my dream. He knew how important it was to me, to be able to dress for a game like everyone else on the team, to maybe even have a chance to play. He knew because I talked about it all the time. All my friends, all my teachers, everyone in the whole school knew how much I wanted it, because I was never good at hiding how I felt about something. If I was excited, you could tell I was excited. If I was upset or frustrated, you could tell I was upset or frustrated. That's just how I was.

On the day of that last game, I couldn't wait for school to be over. The clocks in the school were all moving so slow I thought the final bell would never ring, but then it finally did ring and it was time to get ready for the game. It was the last home game of the season, so it was the Senior Night game, the same Senior Night game that I'd play in and score all those points in a couple years later, only then I wasn't a senior. Then I was just a sophomore. The way it worked was the junior varsity played first. We were playing Irondequoit, one of our main rivals. Then our varsity guys were going to get ready for their game against the Irondequoit varsity, and for the Senior Night ceremony. That's when most of the people were going to come to the gym to watch. For our game, there weren't a lot of people. It was mostly just the parents of the junior varsity players.

JEFF AMOROSO (former junior varsity coach, Greece Athena Trojans)

I remember our team meeting before that last game. We usually met in a classroom. For some reason, Jason was late to the meeting, which was a very rare occasion, so I took the opportunity to explain the situation to the other players. I told them we were going to try to get J in the game, and that I didn't want any of them to treat this as a joke of any kind. I was kind of emotional. I said, "This is going to be a serious thing for him." I said, "He's never had a chance to feel like you guys do. He's never had an opportunity to go on the court and be cheered for in a high school forum like you guys do and almost take for granted." I wanted these kids to take this all in, and see what it was worth.

Then, all of a sudden, Jason sticks his face in the window of the classroom, and I flash the other players a look that says, "Okay, now, just don't make a big deal out of it." And Jason came in and he already had his jersey on. And I asked him, "Are you okay? You ready to go, man?" And he said, "You bet I am."

So we went out and played the game. I think we were up by about fifteen points, with about two minutes left to go. Something like that. I remember exactly how it went, putting Jason in. I stood up, I clapped my hands, I said, "All right, J-Mac, let's do it." And he went to the table. It was a small crowd, in comparison to what happened at the varsity game two years later, but the energy was extremely similar. Everybody in the gym could tell that this was a special situation, and I had nothing organized with the coach of the other team. We just let it happen.

Jason got a couple of touches, but no shots or anything. And then something occurred that surprised me. There was a stoppage in play, and the referee came running by our sideline and whispered out of the corner of his mouth, "You get him the ball, I'll put him on the line." And I said, "No, no, don't do that. Just play the game." The ref knew what was going on. He was just being a good guy, but I didn't want it to happen like that for Jason. We weren't looking for charity or anything. So we come out of the time-out, and sure enough the ball gets swung to Jason, and he catches it at the top of the key and he lets it fly from about twenty-three feet, way beyond the three-point line. He missed everything, but the whistle blew. The referee put him on the line anyway. Maybe it was a foul, maybe it wasn't, but it was close. You could argue it either way.

Jason went to the free throw line, and the tension in the room was just amazing. You could hear a pin drop. Jason got the ball and he dribbled it, over and over. We counted it one time, watching the tape, and he dribbled it close to twenty times. And then everybody just froze. You watch the tape and it doesn't do it justice. As soon as he released his first shot, I remember very clearly somebody yelled, "Get in there!" And he swished it. And he started pounding his chest, and pumping his fist to the crowd.

Remember, Jason got fouled on a three-point shot, so he had two more shots. So again, people are kind of jumping in the stands. And the ref sends him the ball again. Everybody stops while he dribbles it twenty times again. Another one, swish. Now he's pounding his chest and pointing at his father in the crowd. And finally he gets the third one, and it's dead silent again, and he swishes the third one while he's backpedaling out of the way. And he just started pounding his chest and it was amazing. The energy in the room. People were going bananas, and after the game people were in tears, just sobbing at the beautiful situation that it turned out to be. Who knew that two years later, the same thing would happen times a million?

That game was like a highlight of my life to that point. It was the highlight of my basketball career—that's for sure. I don't want to write about it too much, but I do want to say that everybody at school was talking about it, all during the Senior Night game that came after, and all during school the next day. The whole next week, too. It was a really famous game at Greece Athena. Everyone was like, "Did you hear about J-Mac?" So many people were saying they were there, that they saw me make those shots, but a lot of them had to be lying because there weren't that many people in the gym when I got into the game. If everyone was there who said they were there, the place would have been packed. But it didn't matter how many people were there, it was still really exciting. Also, I was really proud of myself. My mom and dad said I should be really proud, but they didn't need to tell me. I was proud already. Josh was proud of me, too. I could tell. It was a big accomplishment, to hit three straight free throws. You have to play basketball to know what a big deal it is. You have to try it yourself. The game wasn't on the line or anything, so they weren't pressure free throws, but not a lot of people go three for three like that. I couldn't stop talking about it, or thinking about it. I think I drove my parents crazy with how much I talked about that game. My brother, too. Not just that night, but every day for a real long time. One of the reasons I talked about it so much was my autism. When I get fixed on something, I talk about it over and over, and this game got stuck in my head. It was stuck in my head in a good way, but it was still stuck.

That's another place where I got a lot of my superstitions, from that game. I wrote about my superstitions already, but this was where a lot of them started. Now before every game I had to eat the same meal I had before that final junior varsity game. Ravioli, green beans, chicken noodle soup, and a cup of milk. I think I drove my mom crazy, having her make me that same meal all the time. Also, now before every game I had to watch a videotape of me shooting those three straight free throws. I'd do this to get me pumped for the game, but also because it was good luck.

At the end of the season, at our awards ceremony, I got a special award for having the best free throw percentage in Greece Athena history. Three for three meant I was shooting one hundred percent. That's the best you can do. Coach Johnson thought up that award for me. He wanted me to have something so I could remember the game and what happened, but I had what actually happened to remember it by. It's not like I could forget something like hitting three straight free throws. But it was a real award. It was a school record, Coach said, and I never thought I'd have a school record.

After that, I had to try out for varsity the next year, because in Coach Johnson's program there are no juniors on the junior varsity. Technically, you're allowed to have juniors on the junior varsity, but every coach has his own policy, and Coach Johnson's policy was that you had to be on varsity or out of the program. He said that by your junior year if you didn't have what it took to play varsity ball, you should probably move on to make room for some other player to play at that level. I think that's a good policy. I think the junior varsity spots should just be for freshman and sophomores, so they can develop.

My mom said I should talk to Coach about playing another year on junior varsity, but I didn't want to be left back like that. It was like being a supersenior for an extra year. It was the opposite of what I thought, and I knew it was the opposite of what Coach Johnson thought. Besides, the other kids in my grade, all my friends, they were trying out for varsity, so that's where I wanted to try out, and when I didn't make it I was disappointed. Sure, I was disappointed. I worked really hard in the off-season and over the summer. I worked really hard because in basketball there's really no off-season. There's always a place to play, and there are always other kids playing and working on their game, so I played pickup wherever I could. Also, I lifted weights at the YMCA and in the weight room at school. One of the things Coach Johnson told me was I'd have to get a little bigger if I wanted to make varsity, so that's what I was working for. That's why he kept the weight room open over the summer, so kids like me could work on getting bigger and stronger. Also, I tried to take at least a thousand shots a day. That was my goal. I started out counting, but I could never keep the count the whole way through. I always lost my place. But I took a lot of shots, I'll tell you that. I shot baskets at the YMCA, at the school gym, and at the hoop in my driveway. All the time, I was shooting, shooting, shooting. One thousand shots is a lot of shots. I know because I tried to count them out, every single day. I don't know how I came up with that number, but it seemed like a good number.

When I didn't make the team, I was disappointed again, but then Coach Johnson asked me if I wanted to continue in my role as team manager, only this time for the varsity. I was hoping he would ask me that, because that's what I really wanted to do. Other than actually making the team as a player, it was the next best thing, and I really wanted to help our team make it to the sectionals. That's the goal of every high school basketball player where we live, to make it to the sectionals, so that became my focus. That's what I wanted for me and my teammates.

On varsity, I did a lot more than just help out at practice and games. Sometimes I'd go with Coach Johnson or one of the other coaches to help scout one of the other teams. They'd look at the schedule and see who we were playing in the next week or two, and see if there was a game we could watch that didn't conflict with one of our games or practices.

KELVIN GOFF (former assistant varsity basketball coach, Greece Athena Trojans)

A lot of times, Jason would come with us to scout a team coming up on our schedule. After practice, Coach Johnson would pick me up, and he'd have Jason in the car with him, and then from there we'd ride to the team we were going to scout. We'd set up a camera. We'd tell jokes. We always had a good time. Coach Johnson called him J-Mac, but I always called him J-Money. To me, he was J-Money, because he's money when he shoots—know what I mean?

Jason did most of the talking, as I recall. He might be autistic, but he has an awful lot to say. He was like a walking high school sports almanac, that kid. He could tell you about every kid who played basketball in Monroe County, and in Rochester. It's amazing, for a kid with autism to be able to do something like this, but he could tell you how many foul shots a kid hit, how many threes. These were the conversations we would have, on the way out to these games. He knew every team's stats, every team's record. And he knew basketball strategy. He really loved the game, and he really understood the game.

I coached at Greece Athena a long time, and I can't think of a kid who loved the game of basketball more than Jason. He came out for the team every year, and he gets cut. Any other kid, he takes it hard, but not Jason. You call him in and say, "Hey, it's not gonna work out," and then you offer him the position of team manager and he gladly accepts it. He's thrilled. And he doesn't really understand that he didn't really make the team. Any other kid, there's a shame in getting cut from the team, but that didn't bother Jason. He didn't see it that way. He just wanted to be part of the team.

The summer before my senior year, I worked really hard on my game. Every time Coach Johnson had open gym, I was down there shooting. I really wanted to get ready for the season because I knew this was my last chance to make the team. I also knew that there was a good chance I might not make the team, because there were a lot of good players. We graduated a lot of good players the year before, but there were a lot of younger players coming up. Also, my mother kept reminding me not to get my hopes up about making the team. This was another example of her being a glass-half-empty kind of person. This was just her trying to prepare me for something bad, like she always does. I wrote that about her before, that she doesn't like to see me disappointed, and this was just another example of it.

The good thing was Coach had already told me that if I didn't make the team he would invite me back to be the team manager again, so that made me less nervous about the tryout. It was like I couldn't lose. That's how I looked at it. If I didn't make the team as a player, I would still get to be a part of the team as the manager. I was the only kid in the tryout who could say that, the only kid who knew he was already a part of the team, so that gave me a lot of confidence. It made me feel like I had nothing to lose.

I thought I played pretty good at tryouts. I thought all that practice and all that time in the weight room would help me make the team, but Coach took me aside one day and said there were other players who were much stronger. I couldn't really argue with him, because there were a lot of good players. He said he noticed a real difference in my game, though. He said he could see all the hard work I was putting in, and that he would like to reward me for it. He was really nice about it. The way he wanted to reward me for it, he said, was to let me dress for our Senior Night game to end the season. He said this was a promise. He also wanted to reward me by letting me play in that Senior Night game. He said this wasn't a promise, but it was his goal. He said he needed to talk to some people about it, to make sure it was okay, before he could promise it to me. He said this on the day he made his cuts, so it was a good news–bad news day for me. A lot of other kids, they just got bad news. Me, I got both, so I was okay with it. My mom was actually more disappointed than I was, because I knew we had a good, strong team, and a really good shot at the sectionals, and now I would get to be a part of it. I knew all the other good teams in Rochester, and which teams had their best players returning, so I knew this could be our year.

The only problem with Coach Johnson's promise to me, and his goal, was that I became really fixed on it. This was another example of my autism making me fix on something. Coach Johnson said for the rest of the season I was always asking him if he talked to the people he needed to talk to about me playing. He said I asked him almost every day. I don't think that's true.

I thought about it every day, and I thought about asking him every day, but I tried really hard not to. Some days I did, and some days I didn't. But it wasn't every day. It was just every once in a while. When I thought of it, I'd say, "Coach, am I gonna get to play against Spencerport?"

And he'd say, "I'm working on it, Jason."

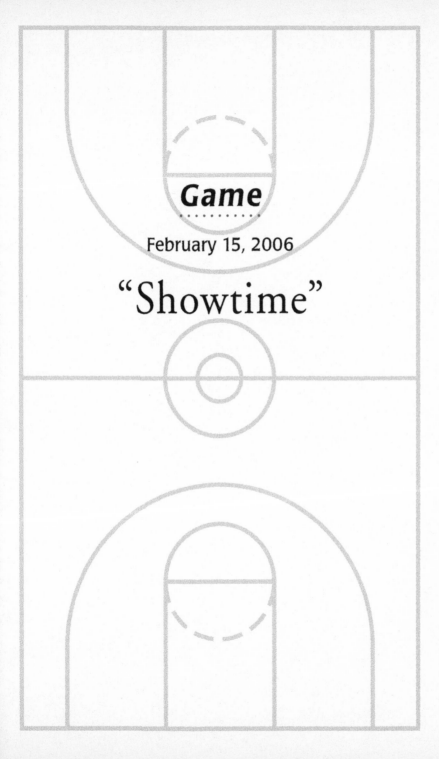

Game

February 15, 2006

"Showtime"

T HE FOURTH QUARTER STARTED WITH the same chanting and clapping that ended the third quarter. It was a really big lead we had now, 50–24, so a lot of people in the gym were thinking Coach Johnson would put me in at any minute. I know my mother was probably going crazy in the stands, worrying when I'd get my chance, but I wasn't really worried. I knew my chance was coming. I knew Coach had already gotten all the other reserves into the game. Also, a lot of the reserves had gotten on the scoreboard, so the guys on the team were excited about that. They were excited about the win, but the game was already decided for winning and losing so now they were mostly excited about their team-mates who didn't get to play too much finally getting a chance to score. And they were excited about me finally getting my turn on the court. I know this because this was what they told me. Who-ever sat next to me on the bench, he'd say something like, "Your time is coming, J-Mac." Or, "Soon it'll be you, J." Or, "You're gonna put one in. I just know it." This was what my friend Steve Kerr said to me.

We went right into our half-court press, even though we had a big lead. This wasn't bad sportsmanship or anything. This was just good basketball. This was just staying sharp and keeping focused. Even though it was the last game of our regular season, and even though we were in control of the game, we still had the sectionals coming up, and Coach didn't want us to change our style of play. We had to keep the pressure on. Not for this one game, but for the playoffs. I think we were a little overanxious to start, because one of our guys fouled a Spencerport player from behind. Unfortunately for Spencerport, their player missed both free throws, and we grabbed the rebound. We missed our next shot, though, and they missed their next shot, and then we traded possessions for a while until Rickey Wallace finally broke free on a fast break for an easy layup, and as soon as the ball went through the hoop the kids in the 6th Man section started up again. They were standing now, up in the 6th Man section. They'd been standing for most of the game, a lot of them, but now everyone was standing, all around the gym. It was an exciting thing to see and hear. Everyone was cheering, all around the gym. Then Rickey Wallace stole the inbounds pass after his layup and was quickly fouled by a Spencerport player. He hit his first free throw but missed his second, and I had the feeling that if he hit both of them the place would have just burst with noise. The crowd was really into it.

Next time down the floor, I started hearing more J-Mac chants again. All different kinds of J-Mac chants. Ones I'd never heard before. Like the 6th Man kids had run through everything there was to cheer about and were making up new things to cheer about, and then all the other people were just following their cheers and adding to the noise and the excitement. It was hard to think they were cheering for me, because I wasn't used to people cheering for me. But at the same time I liked that I kept hearing my name. J-Mac. My basketball name, anyway. My mother says now that she hates all that J-Mac stuff. "J-Mac this" and "J-Mac that." She says she likes it better when I'm just Jason, but back on Senior Night, back in the early part of the fourth quarter when we were putting the game away and everyone in the gym was cheering for Coach Johnson to put me in, I don't think she minded it so much. Probably she was doing all the cheers and chants along with everybody else.

The teams traded baskets for a while—that's what it's called when one team scores and then the other team scores. After that, the Spencerport coach called a time-out. This was different from the time-outs earlier in the game, because now the score was 55–31 in favor of Greece Athena, and there were only about five or six minutes left in the game, so it wasn't one of those strategy time-outs I talked about or even one of those momentum time-outs. It was just a regular time-out, and when we came out of it Coach Johnson made a couple more substitutions. He was giving everybody a chance to play, and everybody was hustling out there on the court, trying to show Coach and everyone in the stands that they could make a contribution. That's what I would have done, if I were them. I'd play like I had something to prove, like I was playing for a spot on next year's team. Always, that's a good strategy, when you finally get your chance to do something. It doesn't matter if it's basketball, or something else. When you finally get your chance, you're supposed to hustle like it really means something. You're supposed to give one hundred percent.

These were the younger players mostly, the kids who would be back next season, and they were all giving one hundred percent.

Brian Benson, my good friend from down the street, was one of the players out there hustling. He was just a tenth-grader, but he was one of the bigger kids on the court, and he was getting a lot of rebounds. When there was less than five minutes on the clock, one of our guys stole the ball and went in for a wild layup, and Brian grabbed the offensive rebound and made an easy put back to make the score 57–31 in favor of us, and he pumped his fist like it was a game-winning shot. It really wasn't, but it was a big shot for Brian to make, a statement shot. It showed Coach Johnson and everyone else in the stands what he could do.

After that shot, Coach made another bunch of substitutions, only I was still on the bench. I didn't mind, but the 6th Man kids, I think they minded. Anyway, they noticed. They started up with their chanting and cheering again. My dad told me later they sounded impatient, but maybe that's just how it sounded to my dad, because he was getting impatient. He wanted me to get into the game already. There wasn't a lot of time left, and we were up big, and this was what Coach Johnson had promised. Technically, it wasn't a promise. He was very clear about that. But it was a goal. It was something he said he wanted to do. He said if we had a lead and if everyone else had gotten into the game, it would be my turn.

And then, finally, it was. There was a foul called and the clock was stopped. It said 4:19. The scoreboard said we were up 59–31. Coach Johnson looked down the bench to where I was sitting. I was the first player on the bench, so he didn't have to look too far. He said, "Jason, you're in."

I stood up and went to the scorer's table, and the place went crazy. Wild, nuts, crazy, whatever you want to call it. I didn't think it was possible for all the cheering and chanting to get any louder, but it got louder by a whole lot. Also, as soon as I stood up, the 6th Man kids pulled out these pictures they had of me. All different pictures, in all different poses. There was one of me smiling. There was one of me cheering. There was one of me looking focused. One of the parents who worked for Kodak had taken the pictures and had them blown up and mounted on sticks, and now the 6th Man kids were holding up the sticks in front of their faces like masks. They were jumping up and down, all these different pictures of me, and some of the other kids had J-Mac signs they were holding up, too. There was a J, an M, an A, and a C. They were supposed to be all in a row, to spell out my name, but in all the jumping up and down everyone was moving around and some of the letters were out of order. Sometimes they spelled out my name and sometimes they spelled out nothing.

It was funny and kind of weird, all at the same time. I was smiling and laughing, and at the same time trying not to smile or laugh. I was trying to focus, but it was hard to focus because of all the noise and the cheering. Also, I had never seen so many pictures of myself all in one place. There were like thirty of them, all spread around the corner of the gym where the 6th Man kids were sitting. They'd known about this all along, all the other kids. Probably the guys on the team knew about it, too. They'd set it up. But it was supposed to be a surprise. I wasn't supposed to know about it until I got on the court, and when I did finally step on the court it was funny and weird to see my head bouncing up and down on all these sticks. There was also a standing ovation. My dad was probably the tallest guy in the gym, and he was standing. He was so tall I could spot him easily from the court. My mom was probably standing, too, but she's a lot shorter than my dad. She's, like, really short, so I couldn't see her, but I'm sure she was right there next to him, standing and cheering, just like everybody else. She was probably wishing everyone would sit down so she could see better.

Spencerport had the ball when I checked into the game, but then they called a time-out, and during the time-out they started to play this song called "Cotton-Eyed Joe" on the public-address speaker. It's one of those clap-your-hands, stomp-your-feet kinds of songs. It's another one of our regular songs they always play at our home games, and every other time they played it I'd clap my hands and stomp my feet, only now I couldn't really clap my hands and stomp my feet because I was in the huddle for the time-out. It was my job to listen to Coach and to focus on the final few minutes of the game, not to clap and stomp and dance to some time-out song. So on the inside I was smiling and laughing and clapping and stomping, but on the outside I was focusing and concentrating and thinking about what we had to do to keep Spencerport from getting back into the game.

The first time we had the ball after that time-out, Brian Benson set a screen for me down low, in the right-hand corner, just in front of our bench. I didn't know it, but some of the guys had talked about trying to set me up for a shot, hoping to help me get a basket, and right away Brian set me up for a wide-open three. He set the screen and made the pass, and I fired up the biggest air ball you'd ever want to see. I missed the basket by about three feet. It was probably the worst shot I'd ever taken, and Spencerport grabbed the rebound and hustled down to their end of the court, and one of our guys grabbed the rebound and pushed it back up the floor. It was almost like a fast break, but not really. We were pushing the dribble, and I took a pass at the top of the key and drove the left side of the lane toward the basket and put up a left-handed hook that hit the back of the rim and bounced away. For a second, I guess it looked like it was going in, because when the ball bounced away the crowd said a big "Ohhhhh." It was like a giant wave of disappointment that crashed across the whole gym, like everyone was hoping for the shot to fall, me and my parents probably most of all.

Spencerport missed on their next turn down the court, and we grabbed the rebound and came right back at them, this time with one of the guys finding me for another open look. This time, the kids in the 6th Man section were chanting, "Let's go, J-Mac! Let's go, J-Mac!" This time I was in the right corner again, right in front of our bench. I could hear some of our guys on the bench saying, "Take a shot." Or, "Put it up." But they didn't have to tell me. I fired up another three, and this time the ball rattled the rim and went in.

Man, the gym just burst with noise. Everyone was jumping up and down, and all these J-Mac masks were jumping up and down, and the guys on the bench were jumping up and down, and me and my teammates on the court were jumping up and down. It's like I'd won the Super Bowl and the lottery and the Slam Dunk competition all at once.

The scoreboard said it was 62–31, with 3:09 left to play.

I think I lost my focus a little bit after that because I was a little slow getting back on defense. I was caught in this giant, sudden celebration, and the Spencerport player I was supposed to be guarding beat me by a step or two into the corner, and I ended up fouling him as he went up for a shot. It was a stupid foul, but

I don't think anyone in the gym cared except me. I liked that I had scored and everything, I liked that everyone was all happy for me and everything, but I didn't like that I'd gotten beat at the other end of the court.

But like I said, it didn't really matter to anyone else. Maybe Coach would say something to me about it after the game, just to remind me to keep my focus no matter what was going on off the court. It was a good lesson, a good thing to remind me about. But for now I just drifted to center court while the kid I fouled stepped to the line to take his shots, and I tried really, really hard not to smile or laugh or clap or pump my fists into the air or any of the things I felt like doing to join in the celebration that was going on in the stands.

Five

NEVER GIVE UP

THIS IS WHERE THE STORY of the game runs into the story of my life, and now I'll start telling what happened in the last few minutes of that Senior Night game in the same way I've been telling the rest of the story. For this part, I'll let some other people say what they have to say, because I was out there on the court when it happened and busy playing basketball and there was a lot of stuff going on that I didn't know about at the time. Also, there was a lot of stuff my friends and family were doing and seeing and thinking that I didn't know at the time, so this way I can let them tell some of these other things.

First I want to tell a little more about how superstitious I was, because that leads up to the Senior Night game. If something good happened after I did a certain thing, I tried to do that same certain thing over and over again to make sure that same something good kept happening. For a while during my junior year, the first year I was team manager on varsity, I had to wear the same gold tie to every game, and it worked until the postseason, when we lost to Greece Arcadia in a real heartbreaker. After that, I wore something else. During my senior year, I wore a white shirt and a black tie in the beginning of the season, but then we had a two-game losing streak so I switched to a white shirt and gold tie and we won that game, so I wore that up until we played Webster Thomas, but we lost that game, so for the rest of the season I just wore the white shirt and black tie that got us through the sectionals. Every game before the Senior Night game, that's what I wore, and every game after the Senior Night game, that's what I wore.

My brother, Josh, used to bust my chops about my superstitions, because he didn't think that what I wore or ate had anything to do with how our team played in the game.

JOSH McELWAIN

Yeah, I used to bust his chops, but not because he was autistic. This wasn't the autism making him do the same thing the same way every time. This was just stupid. So I tried to break him of that. If I was home, I'd hide his tie or that tape of the j.v. game, and he'd run around the house, getting all frantic, saying how the team was going to lose because of me. But he got so upset about it that I'd finally just give him whatever he was looking for, and after that he was okay. After that, if we didn't win, it was because it was time to change the tie or something. Like I said, it was stupid.

Going back to right after I got into that Senior Night game, right after I hit that first shot, it's like my season was complete. And it wasn't just my season. It was my whole high school career. That's all I ever wanted, to get into a varsity game and get a chance to score. That was my dream. A lot of people, they said it was an impossible dream, but I never gave up on it. That's one of my mottos, to never give up, even if it's an impossible dream. And on top of that, to have a chance to win our division and then to go on to the sectionals, that was more than my dream. That was everything. That was what we were working for the whole season. That's why I kept wearing that white shirt and black tie, because it was working, and because I wanted to do everything I could to help my team.

The only problem after I sank that first three-pointer was I felt bad that I lost some of my focus and forgot to get back on defense. In basketball, it's what they call a lapse. I had a lapse on defense, and I felt bad that I fouled that Spencerport player as he was going up for a shot, and even worse when he made his two free throws. Not bad like embarrassed or anything, but bad like I was mad at myself, bad like I'd let my team down and wished it didn't happen. Nobody likes to get beat like that, especially when there's a gym filled with people cheering for you. You go from high to low in just one possession and it doesn't feel very good. You feel like everyone was counting on you and you didn't do whatever they were counting on you to do. The people in the stands were still cheering for me when it happened. Probably a lot of them didn't even notice, since they were so busy cheering and jumping around, but it's like I gave back that shot I'd just made from the corner, so as soon as we got the ball on the inbounds play and I got a pass near the top of the key, I moved to my left for another open jumper, this time out on the left wing. I wanted to put those points back up on the scoreboard, the ones I'd just given back. This time, my foot was on the three-point line, so it was only a two-pointer, but the ball went in and the people went crazy all over again and I was happy all over again and I stopped feeling like I'd let everyone down. This time it was a straight swish, nothing but net. I went from low to high, just like that, in one possession. I felt good because it erased the points I'd just given to Spencerport with that shooting foul. It put me back to even. Actually, it put me back to three points ahead, because that first shot was a three-pointer.

As I dropped back on defense I thought, *Okay, now I've got my points.* I thought, *Now I can just concentrate on playing good defense and helping Greece Athena hang on for the win.* We still had the sectionals to think about, coming up. We still had to finish this game on a strong note. We still had to keep our focus, and work on some things we needed to work on to get ready for the next game.

But there was another problem. It was hard to keep our focus with all the noise and excitement going on in the gym. Anyway, it was hard for me. I don't know how other players do this when it happens to them, how they concentrate on the game, because the people in the stands were yelling down to me, trying to get my attention, trying to congratulate me. Even the other guys on my team were calling out to me from our bench, saying stuff to me as I passed. The NBA players, I don't know how they do it either, because fans probably yell stuff at them all the time, trying to get their attention. Anyway, I couldn't really concentrate the way I wanted to. There was too, too much going on.

Spencerport answered with another field goal, so we were back to trading baskets, and once we got the ball on offense my teammates started looking for me again. I didn't notice it at the time, but they were only looking for me. It's not like they had a meeting about it or anything. It's not like Coach Johnson sat them down before the game and said, "Hey, if J-Mac gets in I want you to only look for him." It's not like the captains got together and decided this was what they were doing. That's not what happened. But I watched a tape of the game afterward, and each time down the floor my teammates were looking to set me up for a shot. I think it was just an unspoken thing. Or maybe it was something they thought up on their own, individually, and it just happened naturally. If you ask me, that's what I think, but however it happened, the whole time I was in, all four minutes and nineteen seconds, no one else on Greece Athena even attempted a field goal, so the ball came to me every time. The other guys on the floor looked for me every time. Whoever had the ball moved it around on the perimeter until I was able to break free from the guy who was guarding me, or they drove the lane until the defense collapsed on them and they kicked it back out to me, and on this next possession I ran behind a screen to get open in front of our bench again, and fired up another three as soon as I got my hands back on the ball.

JIM JOHNSON

The first time Jason shot the ball, coming off that screen, he missed so badly. It wasn't like him, to miss so badly. He missed about six feet, left. And the interesting thing, when you're in a high school gym and you see a shot like that, the kids all yell out, "Air ball!" I thought,

Oh, no, I hope they don't get on Jason for that one. And to everyone's credit, they didn't. You didn't hear anything, so from a sportsmanship perspective, that was great. There was just a hush. Our kids wouldn't have yelled anything, of course, but the Spencerport fans, they would have made some noise about it. But everyone was just quiet.

My heart sank for Jason, but he was fearless. He came out gunning. This was one of those times where the autism probably helped. It's weird to say this, but he was so completely focused on scoring that nothing else seemed to bother him. He was in such a zone. That's just how he is. Typically, when you put a kid in the game like that and he shoots an air ball, he's very apprehensive to shoot again, from embarrassment. But Jason doesn't get embarrassed. This just rolled off his back.

He missed his second shot, but then he came back and hit his third. A three-pointer, more toward the wing than the corner, right in front of our bench. The place just went bananas. My guys on the bench, the kids in the stands, the parents, everyone.

I couldn't have been happier for Jason. Really, I was just thrilled. My first thought was, *Oh my God, my dream for him has come true.* I was fighting back tears—that's how happy I was for Jason. But then my next thought was, *Okay, one and done. He got his three. Let's move on.* I wasn't thinking of taking him out, but I wasn't worried about getting him the ball after that. And yet his teammates kept getting him the ball. My dream for him had been to score, that's all, but I didn't tell the team that. I

didn't tell Jason. Everyone just figured it out for themselves. That's what will always be special, how these guys
kept setting Jason up. For the rest of the game, they kept
getting him the ball. No one else took a shot, so again
from a sportsmanship perspective, that was great. You
have to realize, these were guys who didn't get to play a
lot, guys who didn't get a chance to put their own points
on the board, and they were giving up open looks to
keep getting Jason the ball.

I was really feeling it. If you've ever played any kind of basketball, at any level, you'll know what that means. When you're
really feeling it, it means that everything you throw up somehow
goes through the hoop. It means you have some kind of magic
touch. It means you're shooting without really thinking about it
and it feels like you can't miss. It gets that way sometimes. It gets
the other way sometimes, too, where everything you throw up
misses wide or deep and it feels like you'll never make another
basket again, but I'd just hit three long-range jumpers in a row
and it felt to me like I couldn't miss, like I could put a blindfold
on and still make the shot. So, yeah, definitely, I was feeling it,
and the kids in the stands were feeling it, too. That's how they
talk about it in basketball. That's what they say when you're hot.
Kids, parents, teachers . . . it was like everyone in the Greece
Athena gym was feeling it, and pulling for me to do well. I remember wishing my brother, Josh, could be there, to see me hitting that last three. He was the reason I started playing basketball
in the first place, so when this last three went in that's what I
thought about. He couldn't come because he was away at school,

and there was supposed to be a bad snowstorm coming and my parents didn't want him driving back to Rochester in a bad snowstorm. Otherwise, he probably would have come.

People asked me later if I knew how many points I'd scored, how many baskets, and it was hard to give a good answer. Usually during a game, I could tell you how many points my friends had. If you came to me during a time-out, I could tell you how many points Steve Kerr had, for example. I just kept a running count in my head, all during the game. I couldn't keep it for everyone, but I could keep it for my friends, and for most of our main players. I could even tell you how many fouls they had, and sometimes even their free throw percentage, like if they were four for five or something. But with me out there playing, I couldn't really tell you how many points I had without stopping to figure it out. I could tell you about each shot. I could tell you about the first three-pointer from the corner, and the second field goal with my foot on the three-point line, and this last three-pointer from in front of our bench, and then I could add it all up and come up with eight points. But I couldn't tell you the total off the top of my head. So the answer I gave was that I didn't really know how many points I had at the time, which was the truth. I wasn't keeping count. All I knew, really, was that I had hit a couple shots and that we were up big and that it was a good night for the Greece Athena Trojans. That's all. It was only later, after thinking about the game, and going over each possession, and looking at the tape, and trying to remember everything that happened during those last few minutes, that I was able to keep a running count.

Next time down, I called for the ball at the top of the key and took another three-pointer. I never thought of myself as a ball hog or anything, but I just kept shooting and shooting. I kept calling for the ball, too. I don't know why. I was really feeling it, I guess, like I explained. Someone said later I was playing with a lot of confidence, but I don't think I was playing any different than I usually played. I was just playing, but this one didn't fall. This one hit the rim and bounced away, and I could hear the 6th Man kids say another "Oh!" It came out sounding like another giant wave. Like everyone was disappointed that the ball didn't go in, all together, all at once. Probably there was my mom's voice in there, too, saying, "Oh!" along with everyone else. Probably there was my dad's. But I couldn't pick them out with all the noise.

The disappointment didn't last for long, though, because we grabbed the offensive rebound and the ball came back out to me, and then I put the ball on the floor and drove the lane for a layup. I had a good look, but the ball didn't fall, and there was another cry of "Oh!" from the stands, another giant wave of disappointment. It was like being at a movie, where the audience reacts at the same time to whatever's going on, and says the same things, like they're reading from a script, only here me and my friends on the team were inside the movie. Here the people in the stands were watching us, and reacting to us. To me. I never really thought about it until just now as I'm writing about it, but I don't think I'd ever been on the inside of what everyone was watching before.

BRIAN BENSON

We kept getting Jason the ball. That was the main thing. We weren't looking to show up Spencerport or anything, or to pile on the points, but Jason was hot. This was a once-in-a-lifetime thing. Nobody had to tell us what it meant. Nobody had to tell us what to do. We got the ball, we looked for Jason, that's all.

After the game, Coach Johnson said Jason was as hot as a pistol, and Jason heard that line and started using it himself. Whenever he was interviewed about the game, he'd say he was as hot as a pistol. It got to be kind of a joke, that line. It was funny, the way he kept repeating it, but it was true. He was as hot as a pistol.

I don't think any of us had any idea how many points he had. He just kept hitting his shots, and we just kept getting him the ball. He'd hit another three, and I'd drop back on defense and flash this look to the guys on the bench, like we couldn't believe what was happening. It was unreal. They were jumping up and down so much on the bench I thought they'd kick the chairs over, that's how excited they were. We were jumping up and down, too, on the court, but there was still a game going on, so we couldn't get too excited. There were a couple misses in there, but even when Jason missed, it's like it was just a matter of time before he hit another one. It's like we knew he wasn't done.

Spencerport grabbed the rebound, so I hustled back on defense. I didn't want to get beat again, but I didn't have to worry about that on this possession because someone else's man fired up an air ball. My friend Brian grabbed the rebound and we pushed it back up the court, and as we crossed the half-court line I could hear the people chanting, "Let's go, J-Mac! Let's go,

J-Mac!" That doesn't happen a lot, that people cheer for you. Most people, they probably never get to hear it, but now I'd heard all different kinds of cheers with my name in them. It was pretty cool.

One of my teammates found me down in the right corner again, and without even thinking about it I put up another three. I was just shooting and shooting. Lucky for me, it went in, and everybody went crazy. Actually, they'd already gone crazy, so they went crazy on top of crazy. Completely crazy, I guess you'd call it. Coach Johnson called it "bananas." That's the word he used. In a lot of the interviews he gave after the game, he said people went bananas. Whatever word you use for it, there was a lot of jumping up and down and yelling and high-fiving. The guys on our bench were standing and hugging each other like we'd just won the sectionals. The guys on the court were jumping up and down, like they were going for fake rebounds. Even Coach Johnson was clapping his hands together, only not a lot. He wasn't going nuts or anything, not like everyone else, because he was the coach and he had to act a certain way, but I could see he was smiling. Inside, he was smiling, and also outside, a little bit. He wasn't standing, though. Usually, during a game, he's standing the whole time, like I wrote about, but during the last few minutes of this Senior Night game, he just sat and smiled. A lot of times, he had his hands over his face, like he couldn't believe what he was seeing. Almost everyone else in the gym was standing, it seemed, and when you're down on the court, looking up at all those people standing, the gym seems a million times smaller, a million times more crowded. And it seemed a million times louder, too, with the way everyone was screaming and calling out my name. I thought the bleachers would collapse, because everyone was jumping up and down so hard. You could actually see the bleachers shaking. You could also see those couple dozen J-Mac pictures, floating above the crowd on sticks. And the J-M-A-C letters, which sometimes spelled M-J-A-C or A-M-C-J, depending on where everyone was moving in all the excitement. That was the strangest part, to see my face all over the gym, to see the letters that were supposed to spell out my name, but it made me feel good.

That made it eleven points in just under two minutes, and we were back to doubling up the Rangers, 70–35. I always liked it when we doubled up on the other team. It meant we were dominating the game. It meant we were in control. It was one of my favorite things, to look up at the scoreboard and see that we were up big, so I looked at the scoreboard again. It was up high on the wall behind our basket. Then I hit another three, a sweet shot from the wing on the right side. This was one of my favorite shots of the whole night because it was such a quick release. It really was sweet. Just like I practiced it, all those hours on my hoop in the driveway. Just like I pictured it in my head, when I let the ball go. Just like Coach Johnson has us do in the catch-and-shoot drills he used in practice. The Spencerport players were guarding me a little closer each time I touched the ball, so I knew I had to get off a shot right away, so I just snapped my wrists and followed through, without even thinking about it. I was really feeling it again. It went away for a shot or two, but now it was back, and we were up 73–37, and there was so much noise I thought things would start to fall from the ceiling.

There was less than a minute to go in the game now and the 6th Man kids had basically spilled onto the court. They were everywhere and all around. There were teachers and security people and even some parents trying to push them back onto the bleachers, but they were lining our side of the court like they were at a parade, like they were pushing their way into the front row for a better look. Some of them were actually on the court. Not on the out-of-bounds part of the court, but in play. If the refs wanted to be strict about it, they could have called us for a technical foul, because we were the home team and we were supposed to control our home crowd, but they weren't too strict about it. They were caught up in the excitement, too, I guess. Of course, if the ball went out and we had to set up an inbounds play, it would have taken a couple minutes to clear the area and get everyone back up into the stands. Probably if the game was close the referee would have called an official time-out and made everybody take their seats, but it wasn't close so we kept playing. It was like one of those games you see on the highlights on ESPN, where some amazing stuff happens and everyone is all excited and you wish you were there.

On the tape, you can see a lot of the faces in the stands, and everybody who watches it notices that almost all of the people in the gym were smiling. Even the Spencerport players and the Spencerport parents, you can see them when the camera turns to shoot the whole gym, and even they look like they're smiling. I knew they were Spencerport people because they're the people I didn't know, the faces I didn't recognize. Someone explained to me that this is because this was a feel-good moment. This was one of those times where winning and losing didn't really matter. The winning and losing part was already decided, so this was just a bunch of people feeling good and happy for a kid who didn't get a chance to play finally getting a chance to play and show the whole town what he can do. A kid with autism who used to sit by himself in the corner, banging together two packs of Trident gum and rocking back and forth and not talking. A kid like me. Anyway, that's how everyone explained all the smiling, but I have to say that winning and losing did really matter. It mattered to me, and it mattered to my teammates. All these three-pointers, they wouldn't have mattered at all if we weren't winning, and you can also see on the tape how I was out there on the court, trying to get my teammates to keep focused, trying to make sure we were matched up on defense. You can see all the people jumping up and down and smiling and cheering, and you can see me down there on the court, worrying about the game. That's really how it was. It didn't matter that we were up by thirty-six points. It didn't matter that there was hardly any time on the clock. We still had our jobs to do.

DEBBIE McELWAIN

I just couldn't believe it, what we were seeing. My husband, Dave, and my son Josh tell me I worry too much about Jason, and I suppose that's true. I don't want him to get his hopes up about some things, to put himself in a position where he might get disappointed. That's what I was thinking before this Senior Night game. That's why I told Jason not to get his hopes up about getting into the game. I told him that maybe Coach Johnson wouldn't be able to do it. But then he does get into the game and what does he do? He starts making all these baskets, and everybody is cheering for him, and it was such a wonderful, wonderful thing.

You can't imagine what it's like, to be the mother of a child who was diagnosed as severely autistic as a toddler,

to struggle with him the whole way through all his doctors' appointments and his special-education classes and
his autistic outbursts and all the other things that had to
happen differently for him, to see the disappointment on
his face as he watched the other kids do the things he
couldn't do, and then to have this one great moment
where we could all just close our eyes and think he was
like everyone else. Really, you can't imagine it. I wanted
to jump from my seat and run down to the court and hug
Coach Johnson and the other coaches and the other boys
on the team and everyone in that gym, really, for helping
Jason to experience something like this.

I hit another three, right in front of our bench. My friends
were all saying stuff to me, and sticking out their hands for me to
high-five them or fist-pump them before I dropped back on defense. I was caught between wanting to celebrate with them and
wanting to keep my focus, so I did a little of both. I slapped their
hands and pumped my fist as I ran back down the floor to pick
up my man. I think I might have even pounded my chest once or
twice, like you see the pros do on television, but at the same time
I was hustling down the court because I didn't want to get beat
again.

I didn't know it at the time, but that last shot put me at seventeen points. Five three-pointers and that two-pointer with my
foot on the line. Six for ten overall, including five for eight from
three-point range. That's a lot of shots to get off in a really short
stretch of time, but that's how the game was going when I checked
in. That's how we were playing Spencerport all game long. We

were getting our looks and our stops and you could see the result on the scoreboard.

Unfortunately, I missed my next two shots, so for a while it looked like a twenty-point game would be just out of reach. That's always a big milestone for a basketball player, to score twenty in a game. I wasn't thinking I'd score twenty, and I don't think there were too many people in the gym who thought I was close, but I had two chances on this possession. I missed the first one, from the left side, but the ball deflected out of bounds off a Spencerport player and we kept the ball. Then my teammate Mike Long hit me with a cross-court pass on the left side, and I missed another three, and I started to think maybe my hot streak was over. Maybe I wasn't feeling it so much anymore.

But it turned out I had one shot left. Spencerport scored on its next trip down the floor, and I took the inbounds pass at the center circle with maybe ten seconds left on the clock. I pulled up on the right wing, back in front of our bench, and I could hear the guys telling me to put up one last shot. I could hear some of them counting down, the way you do at basketball games when time is running out. They were saying, "Ten, nine, eight, seven, six . . ." Before they got to five, I put up one last shot, and it went in. Another three-pointer. I was way beyond the three-point line for this one. It was like an NBA three-pointer.

There were maybe two or three seconds left on the clock at this point, but Spencerport never really had a chance to put the ball back into play. The crowd of people in the 6th Man corner was too big. They were too crazy with excitement. They just kind of pressed their way onto the floor, like a great big blob, and the next thing I knew there was a swarm of people, rushing across the floor to around midcourt, where I was standing with my teammates and celebrating. Soon there was just a crush of people, another giant wave, only this wasn't a wave of disappointment, this was a wave of celebration, and it moved slowly from midcourt to in front of the Spencerport bench, where even some of the Spencerport players were trying to congratulate me. They were a good bunch of guys, the Rangers. Any time you lose by almost forty points, it's a bad loss, but they were good sports about it. They could have been mad, but I don't think they were. I still see some of them around Rochester, or they come into the store when I'm working, and they always say hello.

Somehow, my mother was one of the first ones to reach me after the game was over. She might have been the very first, I can't remember. Anyway, I was really surprised to see her, because first of all she's pretty tiny, compared to a lot of the kids who were out there on the court celebrating. Second of all, she was sitting in the stands, a couple rows up with my dad and the other parents, so she had to move really fast to get down to me as quick as she did. Probably she started moving toward me as soon as I hit that last three, when there was still some time on the clock. Probably she planned to come out and meet me on the court and give me a hug or something, before she even knew everyone else in the school was planning the same thing. However she did it, she was the first to get to me and she held me real close the way she always does when she thinks there's too much going on. She was crying, but they were happy tears, I could tell. She was smile-crying, but at the same time she was telling me not to cry. I don't know why she said that, because I don't think it would have ever occurred to me to cry at a time like that. People always said I was an emotional kid, and I guess that's true. I used to cry sometimes when we got beat. My coaches always said I wore my heart on my sleeve, and at first I didn't know what this expression meant, but then when someone explained it to me I thought it was probably true. But this was no time to cry. I mean, my team had just won the last game of our regular season. We had a shot at the division. We were going on to the sectionals. It was Senior Night and I had just hit a bunch of three-pointers in my first high school varsity game. Why would anyone cry about that?

MIKE SETZER (assistant varsity basketball coach, Greece Athena Trojans)

One of the greatest moments of that night was watching Jason's mom weave through the crowd to get to Jason. If you watch the footage, you can see her in her lime green outfit right behind our bench. She came down from the bleachers and was standing right behind us. You can actually see her in the tape, and then you can watch her when the buzzer sounds. You can watch her weave through the crowd and get to Jason before anyone else, and give him this huge hug, this tear-filled hug and kiss. And it's extremely touching.

And after that, when the kids hoisted Jason up, his mother was bawling. I could certainly understand that. I was crying. A lot of people were crying. Jimmy [Coach Johnson], he was a mess. He was crying, too. Jason's mother came right up and gave Jimmy this tremendous hug and kiss, and she said, "Thank you so much for what you did for my son. I love you." And it was just so touching to hear her say that to Jimmy.

Jimmy actually sat the entire time Jason was in the game. That whole time, he was pretty much crying. He's an emotional guy, but he never sits during a game. In fact, in the sectionals, we had just enough chairs for the coaching staff and the players, and Jimmy didn't have a chair, but it didn't matter because he stands the whole game. But when Jason went in, he was so overcome, he sat down. He started crying when the kids in the stands held up the signs of Jason's face. Jimmy didn't even know about the signs. Those kids kept them all hidden until J-Mac went into the game. And then, as soon as the signs went up, I got Jimmy's attention and said, "Look at that." And you could just see his eyes welling up right then and there.

After Jason missed his first shot, I looked over and could see Jimmy bury his head in his hands. Later, he told me he said a little prayer for Jason. Right after he missed that first shot. He said, "Please, Lord, let's just get him one basket."

A bunch of the guys put me up on their shoulders and started bouncing me up and down. I couldn't even tell you who it was. I've watched the tape, and it's still hard to tell, there were just so many people all bunched together around center court. It looks like the whole team was in there and I remember looking down from on my teammates' shoulders and seeing my mother looking up at me, and she was smile-crying and looking at me like she didn't want to miss a minute of what was happening. All these kids kept trying to press their way into the crowd, and I was reaching out and shaking hands with people I didn't even know. People I'd only seen in the hallways. People I only knew to nod hello. Pretty girls who wouldn't normally say hello. And then there were my friends. The guys on the team. The kids in my neighborhood. The kids whose phone numbers I had stored in my cell phone. Some friends from gym class. Some friends from my special-ed classes. Some of my teachers. My friends' parents. It was just a great big blob of people wanting to congratulate me, and I was bouncing up and down on top of them, never wanting the celebration to end.

It went on like this for about ten minutes, but it felt like hours. Usually after a game, Coach Johnson has us leave the court after five or ten minutes, and even after a win it doesn't take that long for all the parents and friends to say their congratulations and start leaving the gym. When Coach gives us the sign, we go to the locker room or to our nearby classroom and talk about how things went. Then we change out of our uniforms and head out to meet our parents and friends. Tonight, though, he let us stay on the floor for a really long time. The parents and friends were in no hurry to leave, so Coach waited for the crowd to thin out on its own, for the standing ovation to sit down, but it just kept going. A part of me didn't want it to ever end—I'll tell you that. A part of me wanted to stay on my teammates' shoulders forever and ever, because from there I could look out at all the other people and feel normal. From there they could look at me and not think I was any different from anyone else on the team. I thought, *This is what happens when you're a regular kid and you hit the game-winning shot, or make the play of the game.*

I thought, *This is what happens when you're just like everybody else.*

The public-address announcer came on again and announced that I was the leading scorer for Greece Athena with twenty points. The place went completely crazy all over again. That was the first I knew for sure that I had scored twenty. That was the first most people knew. He also said I'd set a school record for three-pointers, but nobody knows if that's really true. It sounds good, but before Coach Johnson came to Athena nobody really kept those kinds of statistics. It's a record for the time Coach Johnson has been there, though. That means it's a record for at least the past ten years, so that's pretty good. And I tell people it's a record for the last 4:19 of a game, or the last 3:09 of the game, if you want to count from when I scored my first basket. I don't think anyone will ever beat that record, if you want my opinion. That's a lot of points, in not a lot of time.

Finally, about twenty minutes after the game, Coach Johnson led us from the court to our classroom, and we sat around on the desks and chairs and talked about the game. There was a lot of excitement. Someone ordered in pizza and soda for the whole team, so we ate our pizza while we talked. One of our players, Matt Davies, had a brother who was an assistant coach at Webster Thomas, so Matt got out his cell phone and called his brother for the score. That was the only way we could think to get a score right away, the only person we knew who'd be at that game. Matt's brother told him that Webster Thomas had just lost to Hilton. He wasn't too happy about it, Matt said. The guys on Webster Thomas, they wanted first place all to themselves. Anyway, that's how we found out, so we celebrated some more because it meant we were in a two-way tie for first place. Also, there was another game going on that we still had to worry about. Irondequoit's divisional record was 8 and 3 going into its final game against Greece Arcadia, so if they won they would also finish 9 and 3, but we didn't care if they won. It didn't matter if it was a two-way tie for first place or a three-way tie for first place, because we were sharing it anyway. But it was still first place. And first place in Monroe County Division II was nice and all, but it wasn't the main goal for our season. The main goal was the sectionals, and that was still coming up. We'd already clinched our spot, no matter what happened in the division standings, but Coach Johnson said it was like a cherry on top of a great night.

JOSH McELWAIN

My father called me up just after the game ended. He said, "You won't believe what just happened." He told me Jason scored twenty points and that it was the most exciting thing in the world. Exciting for him and my mom. Exciting for Jason, of course. Exciting for the whole school. He told me people were crying and screaming and carrying Jason around on their shoulders. He held up the phone so I could hear all the noise and celebration. He said, "That's for Jason." He said, "All that screaming, that's for your brother."

He was right. I couldn't believe it, but really he was only half right. A part of me was like, *Yeah, okay, so what?* I mean, I knew Jason could shoot a basketball. I knew if he got a chance to get into a game and if he got a good look he could score. But twenty points? That was a little incredible, I have to admit. It's one of the biggest regrets of my life, that I wasn't there. I'll get over it, I'm sure, but for Jason, for me, for my family, I just really feel like I should have been there, you know. A lot of my friends were there. I got calls from them, too, as it was going on, but they were nothing like that call from my dad. His voice was shaking. He was so emotional about it. I was like, *Okay, Dad, calm down.*

A little while later, we learned that Irondequoit beat Greece Arcadia, to make it a three-way tie for first. Hilton finished in second place with a record of 8 and 4, just one game back, which meant that things were bunched up pretty good at the top of the division. These were the teams that would advance into the sectionals. We didn't know who we would play in the first round. Actually, we had already earned a bye in the first round. That's what they call it when you don't have to play and you automatically advance to the next round, so our first game in the sectionals would be a quarterfinal game, and it was for that game that we didn't know our opponent. First there would have to be a "play-in" game to decide who we would play. That's what they call it when two teams play a game and the winner goes on to the first round of the tournament. Our quarterfinal game wouldn't be until Saturday, February 25, which was a week and a half from our Senior Night game, so we had a lot of time to prepare for it.

Right away, people started asking me if I was going to play in the sectionals. That's what everyone was talking about at school. They said I had such a great outside shot that Coach Johnson should put me on the team for good, but he couldn't do that because the rules said you had to play in six regular season games in order to be eligible for the postseason. Sometimes, people would say Coach was making a mistake, because they thought I could help us win the sectionals, but I don't think he was making a mistake. I just thought he was being a good coach, and being fair to everyone on the team. Also, he was just following the rules. We had a lot of really, really good players on our team. We had guys who'd been working really, really hard all season long. It wouldn't have been fair to them if all of a sudden I started to play and started taking away minutes from them. These other guys, they'd earned the right to play in the playoffs. Me, I'd just had a good game. So I went back to work the next day as the team manager, back to keeping the team focused and reminding everybody that our season wasn't over.

I'd had my good game and my three-pointers and my twenty points, but now we had the sectionals to worry about. Now we had a job to do.

FOUR MINUTES THAT CHANGED EVERYTHING

FOR A DAY OR TWO, it was as if Jason McElwain scored all those points in a vacuum. Certainly, the halls of Greece Athena were abuzz with his stirring performance in the waning minutes of his team's final regular-season home game. Certainly, the phone in the McElwain home was ringing constantly with congratulations and good cheer. Certainly, too, anyone who was at the game couldn't help but talk about it, and think about it, and otherwise marvel at what they had seen. It's just that it took a while for the rest of the world to notice.

Later that Wednesday night, Jim Johnson called in the results of the game to the high school sports editor at the *Rochester Democrat and Chronicle*, the same way he did after every home victory. He said, "An unbelievable thing happened tonight. Our team manager, who's autistic, came into the game with just a few minutes left and ended up scoring twenty points."

The editor seemed taken by the story, and Coach Johnson

offered a few more details before hanging up. He thought, *If that doesn't get a headline, I'll be surprised.* And yet—surprise, surprise—the next day he opened up the paper and the lead was all about the three-way tie for first place, and the resulting seeding for the sectional tournament to begin the following week. There was no mention of Jason's performance until the fourth or fifth paragraph, and even then it was just a footnote, an aside. And it's not that the story was entirely without news value: the Associated Press sent out a small article on its national wire highlighting Jason's accomplishment, which was picked up in several newspapers around the country, but Jason's hometown newspaper gave it only a passing mention.

Coach Johnson couldn't believe it. He thought maybe it meant it wasn't such a big story after all, Jason scoring twenty points. Maybe it just seemed like a big story because he knew Jason and he knew what it meant to him and his family. Maybe everyone in town, everyone at school, was just too close to it. After all, the *Democrat and Chronicle* is a major newspaper. They know what's news and what's not news. And it didn't even rate a headline.

Someone popped into Coach Johnson's office and announced that highlights of the game were going to be shown on ESPN's *SportsCenter*, and Coach Johnson's first thought was, *ESPN? It didn't get a headline in our local newspaper, it didn't make the local newscast, so what makes anyone think it'll rate coverage on ESPN?* Plus, he couldn't think how ESPN might have gotten a tape of the game. As far as Coach Johnson knew, he had the only tape. Whenever possible, Coach Johnson tried to catalogue the Trojans' games on tape, so he could go back and study his team's performance and chart statistics, and he usually asked a Greece Athena student to run the athletic department camcorder. Some of the kids did a really nice job, capturing the full game on both sides of the ball. He hadn't even had a chance to screen the tape of the previous night's game, and he had no idea how a copy of it might have wound up at ESPN.

He thought it was just wishful thinking that the rest of the world would care the same way the Greece Athena community seemed to care. He thought the buzz around town would die down soon enough, and that he and his players could turn their attention to their first-round sectional game, which was scheduled for the following Saturday, February 25, more than a week away. In the end, that's what this season was about, winning the sectionals. The Senior Night game was just an exclamation point along the way. It was nice for Jason and his family, and it was a special moment for the guys on the team, and you could probably make the case that it was a milestone event for the school, but even Jason would tell you that the sectional championship was the most important thing. That's what they were playing for, all season long. That's what everyone would remember in the end.

Up at the State University of New York campus at Geneseo, Josh McElwain's cell phone was also vibrating with calls from friends who'd seen his brother play the night before. Everyone back home seemed to want to check in to talk about Jason's game, to offer firsthand notes and color commentary, but Josh couldn't understand the fuss. Well, he understood it, but he didn't buy into it. He'd wanted to be there for his little brother, and he was thrilled for Jason and his parents that things worked out the way they did, but he thought that would be the end of it outside his immediate family. He thought it would be something they'd continue to talk about among themselves, something they'd look back on, but he didn't expect to read about it in the newspaper or hear about it on the news or be recognized on campus as the brother of J-Mac, that high school kid down in Rochester who lit it up during the last few minutes of his last game. That would have been making a great big deal out of something that should have only been a big deal to Josh and his family.

David McElwain returned to work the next day still beaming. A neighbor had called him at six thirty in the morning to tell him about the small article in the *Rochester Democrat and Chronicle*. The neighbor suggested to David that he have the article framed, and David thought this was a good idea. He thought this would be his one souvenir of Jason's wonderful game. He didn't care that Jason wasn't mentioned in the headline; he cared that Jason was mentioned at all. He took the article to work and showed it to everyone in the office. He was so proud. It was all David could think about, the way Jason kept draining three-pointer after three-pointer. He'd looked just like a regular kid out there, like he belonged on the floor with the rest of the team. It was a moment David McElwain would never forget, a moment he'd imagined for Jason's entire life, but never in a million years could he imagine anyone else caring about it in quite the same way. That's why he was so surprised, so pleased about the article, because he didn't expect to see it written about in the newspaper. It was a family moment, shared with the high school community and observed by most of the town. It was exciting and uplifting and all those good things, but it wasn't anything newsworthy.

That's the part he didn't get. It was personal, what happened in that gymnasium. It didn't really belong in the newspaper. A scrapbook would have been more like it, because it was something for him and Debbie and the boys. It was something for the town, too. When he heard there was a videotape of the game, his only thought was to get a copy for his family, to add to their home movie collection. It never occurred to him that it would become one of the most downloaded videos on the Internet, or that footage from the game would be played over and over on national television, or that his son was about to become a household name—or, as J-Mac, a household nickname.

Debbie McElwain reported as usual that Thursday to the dentist's office where she worked as a hygienist, never expecting Jason's game to be the main topic of conversation. She had a long-running dialogue with her patients and coworkers. One thing about working in a dentist's office, there's always time to talk. When you're sitting in that chair, you're a captive audience, and so most of her patients knew about Jason. They knew about his obsessions, and his struggles, and this thing he had for basketball. And to Debbie's great astonishment, most everyone who sat in her chair the next day had heard about the Senior Night game the night before. Word traveled fast, she guessed. Greece could sometimes feel like a small town, with everybody knowing everybody else's business, and on this day the McElwain business had spread like a brush fire. Here Debbie had thought Jason had simply made a fine memory for himself and his family, but what she was getting back was that he had touched something deeper in a lot of people. His astonishing turn on the basketball court seemed to remind people that anything was possible. They took the hard circumstances from their own lives and put them on Jason, and he responded by showing people what can happen if you believe in yourself and make the most of your opportunities. He showed them it was okay to hope, because in Jason's performance was the message, *Hey, if an autistic kid like Jason McElwain can step out on a basketball court and score twenty points in just over three minutes, just imagine what you can do.* To Debbie McElwain, this was both a good thing and a not-so-good thing. It was good because it meant Jason had made a difference. It was good because he mattered. After all these years, he had finally found a point of meaningful connection with their friends and neighbors. It was not so good because now people would want something more from him than he could be reasonably expected to deliver. Now the focus would shift from what Jason needed to what other people wanted from Jason. She would have to watch out for that, she vowed. She'd have to help him keep his balance.

Meanwhile, Jason McElwain himself was the center of attention at school. He'd never been the center of attention before, and he liked it. For the next two days, he was floating on a puff of cloud a strata or two above cloud nine. It was way up there, and it was the most exciting thing to be way up there like that. Pretty girls who had never smiled at Jason now stopped to say hello and exchange cell phone numbers in the hallways. Kids he'd never spoken to had something nice to say to him. Teachers went out of their way to shake his hand, or talk to him about the game, or ask him what he thought about the team's chances in the sectionals. He was like a Greece Athena celebrity. To some degree, this was how it was for everyone on the basketball team.

They had just won their division. They were preparing for the sectionals. They were big men on campus. But this was how it was for Jason most of all. He couldn't walk past an open locker without someone stopping to offer a high five or a pat on the back. And Jason couldn't remember smiling so much in his entire life. If you took all the times he'd smiled and added them up and strung them together, it wouldn't get close to the amount of time he'd been smiling since he hit that first three-pointer. His face practically hurt from smiling so much.

Sometime that first afternoon, the day after the Senior Night game, a Greece Athena teacher named Andy McCormick called John Kucko, the sports reporter at WROC-TV, channel 8, the CBS affiliate in town. He said, "Last night I witnessed one of the most extraordinary performances I've ever seen at a sporting event." Then he said, "There's a tape if you'd like to see it."

John Kucko was intrigued. He called Coach Johnson later that afternoon to inquire about the tape. Apparently, the nose for news at channel 8 sensed something the nose for news at the *Democrat and Chronicle* had missed. Apparently, too, there were several tapes of the Senior Night game that had been captured by various camcorders, but Coach Johnson only knew of the tape that had been shot for him by one of his students. He still hadn't screened the athletic department tape, but assumed it had everything John Kucko was looking for, so he invited him to the school to borrow a copy.

There must have been something in that tape to capture Kucko's attention, because he came back with a camera crew to interview Jason and his mom and Coach Johnson. Highlights of the game were shown on channel 8's Thursday early-evening newscast, along with the interviews, and the report drew such a positive response from viewers that it aired again on the late-night newscast at eleven o'clock. Here again, there was that message of hope and possibility, all around. People couldn't look at footage of Jason's performance without feeling good—about Jason, about the human spirit, about themselves.

By Friday, camera crews from three of Rochester's four network affiliate stations descended on the Greece Athena campus to interview Jason, Coach Johnson, and other school officials. Debbie McElwain was interviewed, too. In addition to channel 8, there were crews from WHAM-TV, channel 13, the ABC affiliate; and WHUF-TV, channel 31, the Fox affiliate. RNEWS-9, the local twenty-four-hour cable news station owned by Time Warner Cable, also weighed in with a report. Rochester's NBC affiliate, WHEC-TV, channel 10, had devoted most of its news resources to the network's Winter Olympic broadcast from Turin, Italy, and so did not contribute to local coverage of the J-Mac phenomenon.

After airing his station's J-Mac report that Friday, WHAM-TV sports anchor Mike Catalana called Coach Johnson to talk about the story. He said he couldn't remember the last time viewers had responded so favorably to one of his reports. He said, "Jim, this is extraordinary. Do you mind if I send it on to the network? They might want to do something with it." As an ABC affiliate station, the "network" also meant ESPN, which was owned by the same parent company.

Coach Johnson said, "Of course not. If I hadn't been there to see it for myself, I would have never believed it."

John Kucko, too, sent his report on to CBS News.

And that might have been that, were it not for the enduringly powerful image of young Jason McElwain stepping fearlessly to the three-point line and firing up long-range bomb after long-range bomb, to the boundless delight of the home crowd, his teammates, and himself.

This was turning out to be a story with legs.

And heart.

Things started to percolate over the weekend. A producer from *CBS Evening News* called, wanting to do a piece on Jason and the game. CBS News reporter Steve Hartman was assigned to the story, and he made arrangements to come to Rochester to interview Jason and the McElwain family and Coach Johnson on Monday morning.

Meanwhile, ESPN showed highlights from the Senior Night game for the first time that weekend, which immediately turned Jason from a local phenomenon into a national folk hero. By Monday morning, when the CBS News crew arrived, there was bedlam in and around Greece Athena High School. Before that, it had just been a kind of controlled chaos. Now it was out of control. There was no school, on account of the Presidents' Day holiday. In fact, there would be no school all that week. The basketball team would practice, to prepare for the sectionals, but the building was otherwise closed for the Presidents' Week school vacation. But that didn't stop the brush fire from spreading. Jason appeared with Coach Johnson on CNN for their first national interview. They went with Jason's parents to the studios of RNEWS-9 for the segment. Jason might have been a bit overwhelmed by all the attention, because he fairly fumbled his way through the live interview. The local news stories had been taped and edited, but here Jason was nervous, and it showed. Coach Johnson said later that he was probably the only person in

America who had any idea what Jason was talking about, and this may have been so, but Jason came across as a sweet, good-natured kid, the kind of kid people wanted to root for. He might have been rambling, and unable to focus, but he was heaven-sent from central casting. He was Rudy and Rocky and Rain Man and the Little Engine That Could all rolled into one. The spotlight loved him, and he loved it right back.

Later that first Monday, February 20, the McElwains received their first inquiry from a Hollywood producer, who wanted to make a movie based on Jason's life and unlikely performance on the court. It was the first call of many. The McElwains had an unlisted telephone number, but a couple dozen callers managed to get through. There were writers and agents and producers and others looking to tap into the J-Mac story in one way or another. There was even a call from a man who wanted to be Jason's bodyguard. David McElwain took that call and thought, *Why would Jason need a bodyguard?*

"I felt bad for people named McElwain who were in the phone book," he said later. "Their phones were ringing off the hook also. Jason's grandmother, Betty McElwain, received numerous calls. One Cleveland radio station called her at six thirty in the morning trying to find Jason. When she told them that Jason was her grandson, they wanted to interview her on the air."

By Thursday of the following week, eight days after the game, *CBS Evening News* aired its taped piece about Jason's performance, along with highlights from the game. The report proved so popular with viewers that it was aired again the following night, in its entirety. One of the CBS producers called Debbie

McElwain to tell her about the second airing and said this kind of thing almost never happened at the network. It had been thirty years, the producer said, since CBS last aired the same piece on consecutive broadcasts.

The next morning, Friday, February 24, Jason and Josh McElwain appeared on ABC's *Good Morning America*, along with Coach Johnson. Charlie Gibson did the interviews. Immediately after the ABC broadcast, there was another interview for CNN, and that was followed by an interview on ESPN's *Cold Pizza*. After that, the group submitted to a six-hour marathon interview for ESPN, for a taped piece that would first air on Sunday morning, February 26, and be repeated several times in the following week.

On TNT, during an NBA broadcast, the commentator Charles Barkley observed that Coach Jim Johnson should probably be fired. Barkley was known for saying whatever was on his mind, which usually corresponded to whatever was on the minds of his viewers. A kid like J-Mac, Barkley said, he's never played before, the coach puts him in the final minutes of the last game of the season and he ends up getting twenty points, that coach doesn't deserve the whistle. Barkley's jab was quoted in newspapers across the country. One of the Greece Athena assistant coaches clipped the quote from the *Democrat and Chronicle* and hung it over Coach Johnson's desk in a good-natured jab of his own.

By the time school was back in session, on Monday, February 27, Greece Athena officials were being inundated with requests for interviews with Jason and Coach Johnson. It got so crazy that Coach Johnson couldn't teach for a couple weeks. The school hired a substitute to handle his gym classes, so he could handle the flood of calls about Jason, and at the same time prepare the team for its run at the sectional title. At one point, Coach Johnson recalled, he had a different phone to each ear and another caller on hold and an assistant coach in his office waiting to discuss an upcoming game plan.

On the SUNY Geneseo campus, Josh McElwain was suddenly moving about in his little brother's shadow. He was like a national phenomenon once removed, the way everyone kept picking him out as J-Mac's big brother, and he thought it was a strange and funny thing, how an abrupt shot of family fame can change things up on you.

On ESPN, Jason's incredible string of three-pointers became like video wallpaper, the network played it so often. It was the Play of the Day, and then the Play of the Week, and it would have been the Play of the Month if they wanted to take it that far. It got so you couldn't point the remote past any one of the ESPN channels without seeing one of Jason's shots, or the celebration after the game, or the packaged piece that had been pulled from that six-hour interview.

For a kid who used to cover his ears at the sound of any sudden, jarring noise, Jason McElwain was making quite a racket. And the clamor wouldn't go away any time soon.

Inevitably, news of Jason's accomplishments reached into the extended mental health community, where all of a sudden autistic children and their families had a role model.

"A lot of us feel like this is our gift, to have this happen and to have it receive so much national publicity," noted Dr. Catherine Lord, director of the University of Michigan's Autism &

Communications Disorders Center, in a newspaper interview. "There are thousands of Jasons out there, carrying the net for the soccer team, keeping statistics for the baseball team, playing the drum for the school band. This serves as a reminder to give these kids a chance wherever possible."

Perhaps the most iconic example of autistic behavior is Dustin Hoffman's Oscar-winning performance as the autistic savant Raymond Babbitt in the 1988 film *Rain Man*, despite the fact that autism is only rarely associated with savantism. Indeed, there is no direct correlation between autism and intelligence. Jason, for example, is also learning disabled, so he struggled to process new information throughout his school career.

According to a 2004 study issued by the Centers for Disease Control and Prevention, autism occurs about once in every 166 births—and, curiously, once in every 100 male births—currently affecting as many as 1.5 million Americans. (There is no known reason to explain the more frequent incidence of autism among males.) Alarmingly, that number is growing, at a rate of 10 to 17 percent each year, making autism the fastest-growing disability in the country. The Autism Society of America estimates that some form of autism could reach 4 million Americans in the next decade. One popular theory to explain the surge is a growing awareness of autism, which has led to an increase in the number of diagnoses and in the number of families seeking treatment.

The specific etiology of autism is unclear. For a time, when the disorder was first identified in 1912 by the Swiss psychiatrist Eugen Bleuler and written up in the *American Journal of Insanity*, it was widely held that the disorder might stem from an emotional disturbance, or from a lack of parental affection or attention. Today, however, it is recognized as a neurologically based spectrum disorder, meaning that it is rooted in nature and not nurture, and that it can affect individuals by degrees, from mild to severe. Autism is now viewed as the most common of the five Pervasive Developmental Disorders (PDD) outlined in the American Psychiatric Association's *Diagnostic and Statistical Manual of Mental Disorders* (DSM-IV-TR), ahead of Asperger's disorder, Childhood Disintegrative Disorder (CDD), Rett's Disorder, and PDD-Not Otherwise Specified (PDD-NOS).

As a spectrum disorder, autism follows no set pattern. It presents differently in each case. Individuals who suffer from autism exhibit a range of behaviors, in varying degrees of severity. Some children on the mild end of the spectrum might demonstrate only slight delays in language and communication skills, and only marginally greater challenges with social interactions. With intensive therapy and general development, some of these deficits can be erased over time. Others on the more severe end of the spectrum might appear unreachable to their parents, or even deaf, despite testing normal for hearing; some seem lost in their own trancelike thoughts as they tap endlessly against a tabletop. In these cases, therapy and maturity might offer no improvement.

Characteristic behaviors of PDD spectrum disorders may or may not be apparent in infancy, although they usually become obvious by early childhood, when parents have an opportunity to compare their child's development to their peers'. While there is no conclusive behavioral or communications test that can detect autism, several screening procedures have been proven effective in diagnosing the disorder, ranging from a simple consultation to a forty-item screening scale administered by a psychiatrist.

Some of the warning signs sought by pediatricians in a well-baby screening test include determining whether or not a child babbles or coos by the age of twelve months; whether or not a child points, waves, or grasps by twelve months; whether or not a child can express himself or herself in single words by sixteen months; whether or not a child can offer two-word phrases without prompting by twenty-four months; and whether or not a child demonstrates loss of language or any other social skill at any age. Evidence of any or all of these "red flag" symptoms does not indicate autism on its own, but the continued presence of such behaviors over a long period will often lead to a diagnosis along the PDD spectrum.

Autistic children can also exhibit any or several of the following behaviors: insistence on sameness and resistance to change; repeating words or phrases in place of responsive communication; tantrums; not wanting to touch or be touched; obsessive attachment to objects or routines; uneven gross and fine motor skills; no real fears of danger; oversensitivity or undersensitivity to pain or loud noises; and difficulty interacting with others. Jason exhibited all of these behaviors, at one time or another. As a child, he was also prone to what his mother called his autistic outbursts, which she worked diligently to control. Whenever Jason lapsed into one of his outbursts, his mother would cup her hands around his face and pull in close, as she did just after his Senior Night basketball game. She would try to melt away the rest of the world and get Jason to focus on her, only on her. The idea was to hold him as tightly as possible. Her hands would be covering his ears. Eventually, he would become still and quiet. Sometimes, *eventually* took over twenty minutes. Sometimes, she would give him Benadryl to calm him down. She had read about this in an article—something about the antihistamine helping Jason to relax to a point where he could get his impulses under control—and discovered that it actually worked.

Meanwhile, there was the Trojans' playoff run, which might have been derailed by all these distractions were it not for the cooler heads and guiding hands of Debbie and David McElwain. At home, Jason McElwain's parents were careful to keep him rooted and to restore him to routine whenever possible. They kept reminding Jason that the extra attention would soon fall away, and that the new friends he was making in school might not prove to be true friends in the long run. They weren't doing this in a glass-half-empty sort of way, but in a reality-check sort of way. They wanted Jason to understand what to expect. They congratulated him on his great game, and told him how proud they were of him, but stressed that there would be other ac-complishments still to come, and other reasons for them to be proud of him. They encouraged Jason to be Jason, and not the fist-pumping, chest-thumping J-Mac that kept turning up on the ESPN highlight reel. They also kept pulling Jason back to what was left of his familiar schedule. Realize, this was a young man who craved routine, and here the media attention and local fan-fare might have easily set him off, but Jason managed to keep his focus. In fact, that was his big thing, to stay focused.

He'd been that way all season long, but now it mattered most of all.

"Gotta stay focused," he kept repeating to his teammates, al-most like a mantra, every time the Trojans got together to prac-tice. "Gotta stay focused." He said this to himself, and to anyone else who cared to listen. And the words rang truer now than at any other time during the season.

Coach Johnson was also careful to restore a sense of order and discipline to his team, and to eliminate the distractions that had surfaced since Jason's twenty-point game. One of the biggest distractions, early on, was the debate over Jason's eligibility for post-season play. This wasn't even an issue, however, because of a state rule requiring student athletes to dress for six regular-season games in order to be eligible for postseason play, so it was never an option for Jason to be on the postseason roster. As such, it was a one-sided debate, with no argument against. And yet, option or no, there was speculation in the Greece Athena community that Jason might be used as some sort of badly hidden secret weapon, coming off the bench to help spread the offense and give the Trojans another outside shooter. Reporters assigned to the J-Mac story contributed to the debate, and lent subtle fuel to the notion that Jason deserved another chance on the court. Indeed, there was a groundswell of pressure on Coach Johnson to put Jason on the team, but it was a movement founded on some more of that wishful thinking that had pushed Jason into the limelight in the first place. The coach couldn't put Jason on the roster even if he wanted to. Besides, Coach Johnson said, it was a one-time deal. His team was set. He'd made his cuts at the beginning of the season. Jason would return to his role as team manager and help the Trojans the same way he'd been doing before his Senior Night heroics.

"I was concerned about all that media attention," Coach Johnson said later. "I had mixed emotions about it. It was a mixed blessing. As a coach, you want the publicity. You want people to pay attention to your program, and to recognize what your players are doing. So on the one hand, this was great. We had four news crews at our practice one day that week. Four! It felt like a mini Super Bowl. But on the other hand, it could get in the way of what you're trying to do. So I sat the guys down, as soon as this story started to get big on us, and I told the guys they were all a part of this. I told them to embrace it, to enjoy it, but at the same time to remember why we were all here. It really was a unique situation."

The Trojans drew their crosstown division rivals from Greece Arcadia in the quarterfinal round of the sectional tournament. This, too, was a mixed blessing. The Titans had beaten up on the Trojans the past two years in the sectionals, knocking them out in the semifinal round in two heartbreaking games. Some of Coach Johnson's players still hadn't gotten over those losses. This year's Trojan squad had taken some measure of revenge, however, winning both ends of their home-and-home regular-season series by a total of forty points. They were clearly the dominant team. It looked like a favorable matchup, based on the teams' current rosters, but it was hard to ignore the recent history. Athena couldn't afford to take Arcadia for granted. Moreover, several of Coach Johnson's players had been on those teams that lost to Arcadia in the past two sectionals, and he didn't want them to lose this game in their heads before the opening tip-off.

There was a lot of pressure on Coach Johnson's players—or, at least, a lot of history. The Greece Athena varsity had been to the sectional semifinals six times in recent years without ever reaching the final round. Jason likes to look back now and compare the Trojans' apparent inability to win the big game to the struggles facing his favorite football team, the Indianapolis Colts.

"That's what everybody said about us," he says, "that we couldn't get over the hump and get to the championship."

There was a shootaround on Saturday afternoon at the Greece Athena gym, and for the first time that week Coach Johnson did not allow any media into the session. For the first fifteen minutes of practice, the team just sat around and soaked in what they were doing, where they were, what was about to happen. Coach Johnson wanted his players to put everything on pause for this one session, to block out everything else that was going on in their lives. Jason closed his eyes and tried to picture what it would be like for his team to win the sectionals. He tried really hard to see it, and to see himself inside of it. He had thought about this since he started high school, but he had never really visualized it until just now. He never pictured what he'd do when the game clock ran out with his team on top. He put the Senior Night game out of his mind and made room for that night's playoff game instead. He had spent so much time in his room at home daydreaming about a championship that the picture of what it might look like came quickly. Also, in the past year, he had spent so much time reliving the agony of that semifinal loss to Arcadia. It left him in tears, that game. Even just thinking about it could make him cry. He cried easily, this was true, but he didn't want to cry again over a team he knew the Trojans could beat. He told himself he would give up the memory of his Senior Night game and everything that came after if the Trojans could just make it to the next round.

The Trojans had the home-court advantage and jumped out to an early lead. There had been no news crews allowed during the afternoon shootaround, but one of the local stations had arranged to put a microphone on the Greece Athena bench to broadcast the sounds of the game, so the media circus continued, but Jason and Coach Johnson managed to keep the team focused on its way to a convincing 66–42 victory. It was another one of those statement games, Jason said later. It told the rest of Monroe County's Class AA Section V field that the Greece Athena Trojans were taking care of business. It said they would not be distracted or denied.

"We really took it to them," Jason said.

Before the game, David McElwain looked around the gym and marveled at all the cameras and reporters. It had been more than a week since his son stepped into the spotlight, but David still wasn't used to it. He said he had never been so nervous watching Jason fill up water glasses before a game, with six camera crews recording his every move. Later, when the McElwains received a DVD of the game, it was appropriately labeled "Greece Athena Trojans versus Greece Arcadia Titans (J-Mac versus The Media)."

Greece Athena followed up that quarterfinal win with another convincing win in the semifinals—this time against a strong team from McQuaid the following Tuesday, February 28. Jason never liked how his team matched up against McQuaid, because they had a couple of really big kids on that team, and a pretty deep bench, but Coach Johnson's half-court press and some solid execution helped Greece Athena to a 52–41 win.

The game was notable because it was played at a neutral site—the Blue Cross Arena in Rochester, also known as the War Memorial Arena. The Trojan players called it the Big House, and it was certainly that. More than five thousand people came out to see the game, a number that was undoubtedly swelled by all the media attention. Most of these kids had never seen a crowd that size, let alone played in front of one. There were local news crews in attendance at this game as well, and here again Jason thought he would trade his Senior Night performance for just one more victory. He could have made this same bargain in his head for the whole tournament, and wish his team's way to the championship, but he thought it would be better to wish for one game at a time. He thought this would be a more focused approach, because his favorite athletes were always saying how you have to take things one game at a time. If you start worrying about the whole season, or the whole playoffs, you can start to lose your focus and get yourself into trouble.

Jason made the same bargain with himself before the finals against Irondequoit, another division rival, only by now he realized that the bargain wasn't costing him anything because the Trojans kept winning and he still kept his memory of Senior Night and he still kept getting all this attention. He was still J-Mac, the kid who made all those three-pointers. It was just something to say, something to wish for. The sectionals championship was the bigger prize, he believed, because that was a team accomplishment. The Senior Night game was a personal highlight, but Jason wanted everyone to know he was a team player.

Nevertheless, the Trojans kept winning, and everyone still knew who Jason McElwain was. That part wasn't going away. It didn't matter what kind of deals he made in his head before each game. He walked into the War Memorial before the finals on Saturday night, March 4, and people he didn't know started calling out his name. Guys with microphones and cameras asked him to answer questions or pose for pictures. Pretty girls called out to him and waved him over to say hello. But underneath the noise and attention, Jason managed to keep his focus. He collected rebounds during the pregame shootaround, and when he sent the ball back out to his teammates he reminded them how hard they'd all worked to get to this place. He pressed them to ignore the news crews and the crowd and just concentrate on the game. He said, "Forget Senior Night. These are the finals. Nothing is more important, so stay focused."

Jason was really intense about it, his friend Brian Benson said later. All during the sectionals, it's like he was a different person, like he was in some kind of sectionals zone, and here before the finals he was more intense than ever. He was like a half-crazed cheerleader.

On that Saturday afternoon, just before he left for War Memorial, Jason received a phone call from the NBA legend Earvin "Magic" Johnson, who was part of a group looking to develop Jason's story into a movie. He said, "I don't want to take up too much of your time, Jason. I know you've got a big game tonight." Then he congratulated Jason on his big twenty-point game. He said, "I never scored that many points in four minutes." Then he told Jason how much he wanted to make a movie about that game. He wished Jason good luck in the game that night, and said he hoped they'd get a chance to meet someday soon.

Jason was fairly soaring after the call. Magic Johnson! A true superstar! Jason could hardly believe that someone like that would take the time to reach out to someone like him, but that was definitely Magic on the other end of the line. Jason would recognize his voice anywhere, and now he would never forget the kind, motivating words to go along with the voice.

Irondequoit matched up well against Greece Athena. The two teams had split their home-and-home series during the regular season. Their coaches were good friends. There were more than eight thousand people in attendance—a record for a game of this kind, as far as anyone could recall. It was a strong rivalry, and a close, hard-fought game. Here again, the half-court press and some solid outside shooting made the difference. Athena won by a score of 54–51, giving Jason McElwain the sectionals title he had dreamed about, putting an end to talk that the Trojans couldn't win the big game, and capping a storybook season for the Trojans that saw them rise from small-town obscurity to national prominence on the back of their team manager's unlikely star turn, and then to go from there to the Monroe County Class AA Section V championship.

"There's nothing like winning the sectionals," Jason said after the game, still showing the same intensity he had at the start of his team's playoff push. "It's what you play for your whole career."

Cut ahead to the summer of 2007. This is the bittersweet part of Jason McElwain's story, because by now his friends and teammates have mostly scattered. Some have gone away to college. Some have stayed to attend local schools. Others have remained in the Rochester area and embarked on various career paths. They talk to each other on the phone, or communicate through e-mail and text and IM, but it's not the same. Most everyone has moved on. Most everyone, that is, except Jason, who has returned to his routines. He's replaced the routine of high school with the routine of work, but he still lives at home, still drives his parents a little bit crazy with his particular likes and dislikes, still eats dinner at the same time each night, still watches the same shows on television, still roots for the same teams, still emulates his brother, Josh, and still works out at the YMCA and finds time to take his shots on a basketball court almost every day.

Understand, Jason did not earn enough high school credits to graduate with the Greece Athena High School Class of 2006. He participated in the graduation ceremony, but he did not receive an actual diploma. He received an Individual Education Program diploma instead. He walked with his friends, but unlike his friends he was not walking in any particular direction. He was not walking up and out. He could have continued as a student at Greece Athena until he turned twenty-one, but as he puts it, he had no interest in being a supersenior. It was time for him to move on, he realized, the same way his friends were moving on. He graduated only in the sense that he was graduating to the next thing. He went from being a full-time student to wondering if he'll ever be able to live on his own to worrying about holding a job.

Together with his parents, Jason McElwain looks up from his reestablished routines and sees a long stretch of same unfolding in front of them. Years from now, they all know, he'll still be working in some version of the same job. He'll still be living at home. His friends will have moved on to the next phase of their lives. They'll start families of their own. His brother, Josh, will be off on his own somewhere—probably teaching math and telling his students how his mother never let him use a calculator as a kid. And Jason will be right here in Greece, going through some of these same motions, reaching back in his memory to relive the games he's written about in these pages. He might land a spot in one of several group homes serving the special-needs population in Rochester. There aren't enough beds to go around, so his mother's got him on a couple waiting lists. Since he was diagnosed as a child, she's had him on these lists, because she knew even then that she and her husband couldn't care for Jason forever. She knew there'd come a time when the best thing for Jason would be to move up and out, although lately, Debbie and David McElwain have begun to think that Jason is progressing well enough that he might someday be able to live on his own. Forget the sectionals. Forget the twenty-point game. *That* would be the true pinnacle, if Jason could harness his abilities and his growing independence and find a way to make it on his own.

Jason works now in the bakery at Wegmans, a regional supermarket chain. This has become the stuff of his days. He works three or four shifts a week, baking bread. He would like to work additional hours, but for now this is his schedule. His mom arranged the job for him when he was still in high school, through one of her dental patients. The Wegmans management was well known in the area for hiring dozens of young men and women with special needs and assigning them to ability-appropriate tasks throughout the store. They stock shelves and bag groceries and sweep the floors. Jason was up for anything when he started, because he's a team player. He said he'd work wherever they needed him. The only restriction was he couldn't work outside. This was his mother's rule. Jason and his dad don't agree with it, but they have to go along with it. Even after everything that's happened, Jason knows that he can't go against his mother. She worries about him, still and always. She worries about him spending too much time in the supermarket parking lot. This cut out a lot of jobs, and the prospect of additional shifts, because Wegmans needs people to collect the shopping carts, and to help customers load groceries into their cars, but Debbie McElwain worried how Jason would navigate his way around all that traffic. "He can cross the street just fine, if that's all he's doing," she says, "but if he has to push all those shopping carts, or if he's talking to a customer and not paying attention, then watch out."

Jason says he enjoys baking bread. There's a certain routine to it, a certain rhythm. He knows the recipe by heart, but it's more than just a recipe. It's knowing how to work the ovens, and how to slide the trays in and out without getting burned. It's knowing the routine. Jason knows how much time it takes from when he puts the pans into the oven to when he takes them out. There's a timer, but he doesn't have to hear the timer go off to know the bread is ready. He likes the way the bread smells when it comes out of the oven. He likes how the smell gets into his clothes. He likes when he gets to take home a loaf to share with his parents. He likes when customers say his bread tastes good. (It does!) He likes when they stop to talk to him about his Senior Night game. He likes it even better when they talk about the sectional championship. He likes that he has a place to go, and that his bosses think he's doing a good job, and that everybody at Wegmans knows he's a team player.

Sometimes, he sees one of his old friends or teammates in the store. This happens often, because everybody in Rochester shops at Wegmans. Or maybe he'll see one of his old opponents. Like those kids from that Spencerport team. He sees some of them around. They'll come by the store, and they'll recognize Jason, and they'll get to talking about that Senior Night game. Some of them even heard about Jason's junior varsity game, when Jason hit those three free throws.

Jason likes these times best of all.

When he's not working, Jason takes classes toward his GED.

His teachers tell Jason's parents that he might never accomplish his goal, that his IQ might not be where it needs to be for him to pass his proficiency tests, but that doesn't stop Jason from working toward it. If he learned anything from that Senior Night game, it's that you shouldn't let other people tell you what you can or can't do. It's like those rap lyrics that open the book, which Jason wrote to sing to his friends and teammates back in high school: "Be motivated in everything you do, if you want to catch a dream."

Some weeks, Jason takes a trip with his mom or dad to appear before a church or civic group to talk about autism. He speaks before organizations that help people with various disabilities. He's even been invited to speak at corporate events and motivational meetings for employee groups. He's traveled all over the country, making speeches. He's met all kinds of people. He doesn't know a lot about autism, but he talks about his own experiences. He uses that speech he wrote with his family. It talks about how important it is to stay focused, to never give up, to always have a dream and to always go after it. People seem to like it. He's given it so many times, he almost has it memorized.

Jason McElwain has been in the headlines ever since that Senior Night game on February 15, 2006, along with his family, his coach, his friends, and his teachers. Someday, he might even see his name up in lights, on a movie marquee. Twenty-five Hollywood production companies called within the first week after the story broke, seeking development rights to Jason's story. The family hired an attorney and a media agent to help them sort through the offers and figure out a next move. Requests for interviews and speaking engagements filled the McElwain answering machine at home. It seemed for a time that everyone wanted to get a little closer to the story, and to meet the young man who had caught the sports world, the national media, the mental health community, and the general public completely by surprise.

By all accounts, Jason rose to the occasion, moving about in the public eye with the kind of ease and charm that belied his diagnosis. Indeed, he emerged as a kind of poster boy for autism, a powerful symbol for what a child could accomplish if just given the chance. He became more comfortable in front of a camera and a microphone. Each time out, he was a little more relaxed, a little more like himself. Together with his family, he wrote a speech that he practiced over and over, to deliver to school and youth and support groups around the country. He found that he could answer almost any question with a line or two from that speech, so it was a big help. He started receiving hundreds of letters each week from parents with autistic children, thanking Jason for giving them and their children something to shoot for. He tried to answer as many letters as he could, but it was hard.

Even President George W. Bush offered his congratulations, making time to visit with Jason at the Rochester airport on March 14, 2006, as he stepped off *Air Force One*. The president later told reporters that he wept after seeing a tape of Jason's final game. The two spoke privately for a short while, and then answered questions from the local media and the White House press corps.

The president asked, "Do you mind if I call you J-Mac?"

Jason said he didn't mind.

Then the president said, "You can call me George W."

"It was an honor to meet you," Jason told the president as they parted.

"No," the president responded. "*My* honor."

In April 2006, the McElwains were guests on *Oprah*, along with Coach Jim Johnson, cementing Jason's place in the pop culture firmament. Later that month, the McElwain family reached an agreement with Columbia Pictures to produce a film version of Jason's story, to be developed by Laura Ziskin, the producer of the blockbuster *Spider-Man* series, and the executive producers Mary Martin and Magic Johnson. Jason was happy that Magic and his partners would be making the movie, because he felt a special connection to Magic after that Saturday afternoon phone call. News of the deal was reported on the front pages of *Variety* and the *Hollywood Reporter*. In the wake of the announcement, Magic Johnson traveled to Rochester to meet with Jason and his family, and to Greece Athena High School, where he spoke with students at length about the lessons of hope and determination in Jason's story. It was a huge media event, but it was also a deeply personal and moving moment, for Jason to meet one of his basketball idols on a kind of level ground.

During a press event to announce the development deal, a reporter asked Jason which actor he'd like to see play him in the movie. Jason answered without hesitation: "Matthew McConaughey."

Josh McElwain, who happened to be nearby during this exchange, turned to his brother and said, "That's a stupid answer. He's, like, twice your age."

Jason said, "So?"

Josh said, "So he's too old. He's old enough to be our dad."

Jason responded that he didn't care. He said he thought Matthew McConaughey would do a good job. He said he liked a lot of his movies, and that he looked like he was a good athlete. Then he told Josh to mind his own business and to worry about who could play him in the movie.

Also in April, Jason received an ESL Federal Credit Union Inspirational Award, and he was honored at the Rochester Press Radio Club "Day of Champions" Dinner. The headline speaker at the dinner was the Indianapolis Colts quarterback Peyton Manning, one of Jason's heroes. Before the dinner, Peyton Manning gave Jason an envelope from the Colts that included an invitation for Jason to work as a student intern at the team's summer football camp. Later that summer, Jason spent a week with the Colts during preseason, helping out in the locker room and on the field, and adding Peyton Manning's cell phone number to his collection. He'll never use it, he said, but it's a good thing to have. When the Colts won Super Bowl XLI in February 2007, Jason thought of his friend Peyton and how good it must have felt for him to finally win "the big one." He knew the feeling.

In July, Jason McElwain's twenty-point game was honored by ESPN with its prestigious ESPY award, for the best sports moment of the year. The other nominees in the category were junior golfer Dakoda Dowd's LPGA tournament appearance in honor of her terminally-ill mother; the George Mason University men's basketball team's run to the NCAA Final Four; and Kobe Bryant's eighty-one-point performance in a game against the Toronto Raptors. Jason said that he never expected to win, that he was simply proud to be in such good company. Just to be considered alongside Kobe Bryant, one of his favorite basketball players, was a special honor. This was what he said to reporters. Privately, he told friends he knew he would win. Deep down, he knew. And deep down, he really, really wanted to win.

In his acceptance speech, Jason said it was the best day of his life. And then, for emphasis, he said it was the best day in the world.

Winning an ESPY wasn't as cool as winning the sectionals, Jason allowed after the moment had sunk in, but it was pretty cool. There were more people watching—that's for sure—and tons of famous people around, but nothing could touch the sectionals. That was the pinnacle. Still, the ESPY was up there. The stuff about it being a special honor just to be considered was just the stuff you were supposed to say so you didn't sound like a jerk. Of course he wanted to win. He just couldn't say he wanted to win.

Jason also made an appearance on Nickelodeon's Teen Choice awards show, accepting a Teen Courage Award from presenter Ashton Kutcher.

And yet with all the attention and accolades and the chance to meet some of his favorite athletes and celebrities, one of Jason McElwain's most cherished honors came close to home, when he was asked to throw out the ceremonial first pitch at a Rochester Red Wings baseball game, where the first three thousand fans in attendance received a "J-Mac" bobblehead doll of Jason wearing the by-now-familiar white shirt and black tie that he wore as team manager. It seemed an ironic postscript, that a young man who spent the first years of his life rocking back and forth, banging together two packs of Trident gum, lost to a rhythm only he could hear, would now be immortalized as a bobblehead doll.

He used to have a lot of these bobblehead dolls, but he gave most of them away. He keeps one or two in his room at home, and he likes to look at them and tap the bobblehead so it bobbles and shakes, and imagine what his life was like before they made a bobblehead doll in his likeness. A lot has happened. A lot has changed. Sometimes, Jason can't believe that so many people have spent so much time and so much energy and so much money just to keep connected to him and his family and his astonishing turn on the basketball court.

"I think it's pretty funny," he says, "the way everyone wants to talk to me now, and before my Senior Night game I was just a kid who was the team manager of his high school basketball team. Nobody wanted to talk to me then. Nobody from the news or from television or from the movies. It's funny and it's cool and it's weird. It's all three things. It's funny because of the bobblehead doll and things like that. It's cool because of all the famous people I've gotten to meet, and all the cool things I've gotten to do, like go to the Colts camp. And it's weird because it's not like I have anything more to say now than I did before I scored all those points, because I'm the same person. I'm still just Jason. But I guess people want to know how I did it, and what it was like to be in the middle of such an exciting game, and how it felt to be a part of a team that went on to win the sectionals, which is almost as far as you can go in high school basketball in New York State. There's a state title after that, but then you're competing with schools of all different sizes from all over the state, so the sectionals is the real championship. That was always our goal, at the start of each season, and people want to know what that's like, to accomplish your goal. They want to know what it means to never give up, even if you have autism. Just because you have autism, it doesn't mean you can't do certain things, or that you can't practice certain things and get better at certain things. It doesn't mean that you have to be one way for the rest of your life. It means you have to give all that you can if you want to be all that you can, like I say in my song. Never give up. Never give in. Be all that you can if you want to catch a dream."

—Daniel Paisner
October 2007

Acknowledgments

My dreams were just like other boys' dreams. I dreamed of hitting a home run, scoring a touchdown, or making a game-winning shot in a basketball game. I dreamed that after my winning shot, everyone would cheer and my teammates would hoist me up on their shoulders and carry me off the court. But really I just wanted to be part of the team, just one of the boys.

When I played sports, I was.

What happened since that Senior Night game is hard to believe, and I have many people that I want to thank.

It's important for all of you to know that I'm not a hero here. I'm nineteen. I'm also autistic. My teachers, the other special-education kids and especially my family are the real heroes. Because of them, I dared to dream.

So here are my thank-yous, and please forgive me if I forget somebody. I want to thank all my teammates and coaches for making me a part of the team, and especially Coach Jim Johnson for putting me in the game. All of my friends—you know who you are—as far back as I can remember, you've always been there for me. Dan Paisner for all of his talent and hard work, as well as Mark Chait and Kara Walsh at NAL.

Everybody at William Morris Agency has been so kind and worked so hard for my whole family, especially Paul Nagle, Mel Berger, Betsy Berg, Mike Eisner, Lon Rosen, Laurie Pozmantier, Nicole David, and Jim Wiatt. I'm also really grateful to our producers, Laura Ziskin, Earvin "Magic" Johnson, Pam Williams, and Mary Martin. We would also like to thank our attorneys, Gino Nitti and John Pericak. But most of all I'd like to thank God, who made all of this possible.

This book is dedicated with love to all of my family, especially Mom, Dad, and my brother, Josh.

Without them my dream would have stayed just that . . . a dream.

Because of their love, my dream has become a reality.

Magic says if you don't dream it, you can't become it.

Never give up on your dream and thanks for reading my book!

—J-Mac

A Special Note
from J-Mac's Parents

by David and Deborah McElwain

There are many people out there who have wondered how such a story is even possible. How could an autistic teenager score twenty points in four minutes during a high school varsity basketball game? How could someone who struggled to tie his shoes even learn the difficult game of basketball? How could you go from barely being able to talk to doing countless television and radio interviews? Most astonishing of all, how does a mentally challenged individual transform into a national icon overnight? Even though we are the parents of Jason "J-Mac" McElwain, questions like these have popped in and out of our heads ever since that magical night of February 15, 2006.

As Jason's parents, we have received a great deal of credit for his accomplishments. We would like to think that we did play a significant role, but we would also like everyone to know that there are many other individuals who have taken part in the raising of Jason as well. Without them, who knows where he would be today? For all the people out there who question how Jason overcame the obstacles, you must know that he had many people in his life who cared about him and who helped him along the way, just as much as we did.

We often wonder what we would have done without Jason's brother, Josh. When Jason was first diagnosed, we went through a roller coaster of emotions. There were anxiety, worry, anger, and even sadness and despair. During these times, Josh was our shining star. He was our rock. He always brought a smile to our faces and made it much easier to deal emotionally with all the uncertainties about Jason and his future that were running through our minds.

What Josh doesn't realize is that he was the most instrumental person in Jason's development. The boys are only eighteen months apart, and once Jason started talking, he would mimic his brother and follow in his footsteps, and as a result, he progressed. We cannot thank him enough for all that he has done for Jason. Without Josh, Jason would never have had a dream, let alone realize it. We are so proud of you and are so blessed to have you as a part of our family. We love you very much.

We were quite fortunate that when Josh and Jason were born, our parents were retired and willing to take care of them while we were at work. We had no idea that Jason's grandparents would have such an incredible impact upon his upbringing.

Grandpa Eddie and Grandma Bernice from the mother's side took care of Josh and Jason the most. Grandma Bernice used to lovingly tell the story about how one day when Jason was old enough to talk, they were walking somewhere together, and Jason looked up at her and asked, "Are you autistic too, Grandma?" She replied with a smile and a hug, "You know, Jason, I think we're all a little autistic."

We know that you are not supposed to have favorites, but Jason was Grandpa Eddie's favorite. He brought sports into Jason's life and sparked his interest. We remember the hours on the phone Jason would spend with him, talking about basketball and football games. During the day, he would take Jason to his health club to swim and play basketball. He was always so encouraging to Jason, urging him on and telling him that he could do whatever he set his mind to. An autistic child needs someone pushing him forward when everything else seems to be against him.

On the other side of the family, Grandpa and Grandma McElwain greatly contributed to Jason's development as well. Grandpa McElwain also loved to talk sports with him. Grandma McElwain loved to play games with both our sons. Whenever Jason would go over to their house, they would always play card games or board games, such as UNO or Aggravation. Playing these games helped build the boys' competitive spirits. I doubt you would have seen J-Mac yelling hysterically at the referees from the bench if Grandma and Grandpa McElwain hadn't been so involved in his growing up.

Grandpa Eddie and Grandpa McElwain have both passed away. Their passing was difficult for both our sons, and it is one of our major regrets that they were not here to see Jason's miracle game and the events that have followed. Ever since we signed Jason up for T-ball, he had this entourage that went to all of his games. His grandparents attended all of Jason's and Josh's baseball games, basketball games, football games, tennis matches, track meets, and cross-country meets. They found great joy in watching Jason play and reveled in the enthusiasm that he brought to everything he did. Had they been there on the night of the big game, watching Jason score those twenty points, we are sure you would not have seen two prouder grandfathers on the face of the earth. We know deep down in our hearts that they were watching from heaven and smiling from ear to ear. We like to think they were acting as his guardian angels that night and helping to guide his shots into the hoop.

Jason and Josh also received a lot of love and support from their aunts, uncles, and cousins. They were always there for Jason whenever he needed them. When both sets of grandparents were not available, Jason's great-aunt Rita and great-uncle Bill could be counted on to watch Jason when we were at work. You can never have enough love or support. Aunt Sheila and Uncle Gary, Aunt Patty and Uncle Steve, Uncle Jim and Aunt Betty, we can't thank you enough.

In 1985, our family moved to a brand-new development in the town of Greece, New York. Within three years we had both Josh and Jason. We were very fortunate that all our neighbors had young children as well and that 90 percent of them were boys. Over the years, all the kids became very close to one another and took Jason in as one of their own. Usually it is a difficult task integrating an autistic child into a group of normal, functioning children, but not with these kids. They were a tight group of friends consisting of Josh, Steve, Mark, Mike,

Brian, Frankie, Nick, Scott, Anthony, and Thad, and they let Jason hang out with them. When Jason first started playing with the boys, we sat them down and told them of Jason's disability. They all just shrugged their shoulders and said they loved hanging out with him. They would play hide-and-seek, basketball, Wiffle ball and football together. Playing with these kids meant the world to Jason, and they all remain close friends to this day.

As Jason grew older, he began to hang out with a few other neighborhood kids, first Brian and then Scott. These three were inseparable. They would play basketball, have sleepovers together, and bike around everywhere. The two of them would come up with Jason to Uncle Jim's cottage each year, which only made the friendships even more special for Jason. It meant the world to both Brian and Jason that they were playing on the same basketball team on Jason's big night.

We would like to thank all of Jason's teachers, particularly his special-education teachers. They were outstanding and really cared about Jason, and they encouraged him to work hard both in the classroom and in life. We want all of Jason's teachers to know that they really made a difference in his life, and there is no question that without all their hard work, dedication and devotion, Jason would not be the young man he is today.

We would also like to thank all of Jason's special-ed classmates, who were friends to him as well as to one another, day in and day out. You became a family and shared in one another's highs and lows, triumphs and losses. This book is dedicated to all of you as well.

Finally, you have to give credit where credit is really due—that is, to Jason himself. He has always been our little "charmer." Once he started talking and interacting with people, his personality started to come out. Jason has always had a way about him that would win people over. People naturally warm up to him. He brings a smile to their faces, which is something you can't really teach, let alone learn. Jason is very outgoing, and he is friendly to everyone. He doesn't really see differences among people. His special-education classmates are just as important to him as his basketball teammates. We could all learn a lot from Jason.

When we think back to when Jason was young, and then think about where he is today, we are truly amazed. Who would have ever dreamed that someday so many organizations and even corporations would be requesting him to speak at fund-raisers and employee events? We watch him walk around like a little politician, shaking hands and speaking to hundreds, sometimes thousands, of people. He has handled all the media attention with remarkable ease. At the same time, he has not let it affect who he is and how he lives his life. Jason, you continue to amaze us each and every day, as you continue to grow and progress. You have surpassed our wildest dreams, and we are so very proud of you.

We would like to send our best wishes out to everyone around the world who has reached out to us, expressing their support and congratulations following Jason's twenty-point game. We would like to thank Mary Martin, our friend and producer. We don't know how we would have handled all of this without you. Above all, our family would like to send out our love to all of the other families out there who have children who are challenged in any way. We hope that our son's story has given you the belief that with love and care anything is possible.